BAYTRIPPER
CHESAPEAKE BAY
Travel Guide

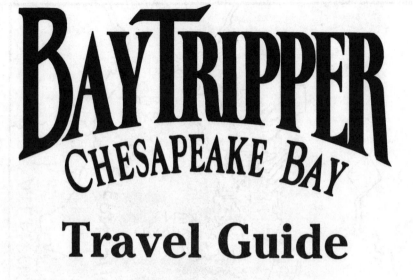

Volume I
Eastern Shore

WHITEY SCHMIDT

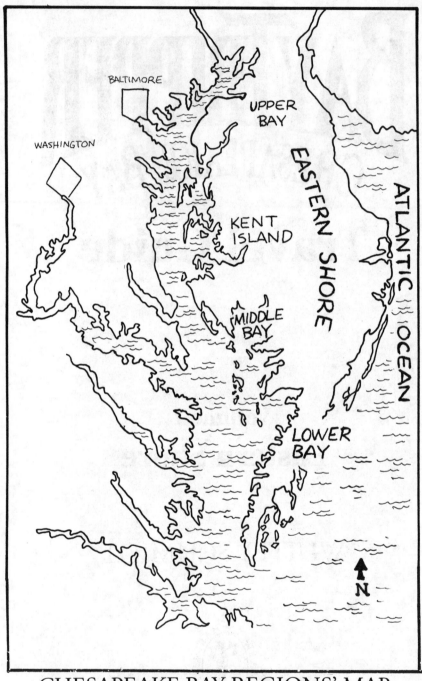

CHESAPEAKE BAY REGIONS' MAP

BAYTRIPPER
CHESAPEAKE BAY

Illustrated by
Craig Robinson

For Matt

Printed in the
United States of America
First Printing 1995
ISBN 0-9613008-1-7

Library of Congress Catalog Number 95-75813
Copyright 1995 by Marian Hartnett Press
Box 51 Friendship Road
Friendship, Maryland 20758

CONTENTS

Introduction/Eastern Shore

Whether you're exploring the Chesapeake Bay region for the first time or returning for another visit, you're in for a treat. I've lived on the banks of the Chesapeake Bay all of my life, and I love it here. About 10 years ago, I moved to a beautiful area approximately 25 miles outside of Annapolis. Where else could I walk a few steps from my home and watch 44 swans meandering off shore? The natural beauty outside my window is ever changing with eagles, osprey, and otters, as well as migrating Canadian geese in the winter. And at the same time, I am only an hour away from Washington, D.C., and all it has to offer.

And there is another reason why I love it here—the fresh crab. Crab cakes and seafood are specialties around the Bay as are the wonderful views to dine by. As a restaurant critic, I've sampled the offerings of many of the varied restaurants in the region. All of my books are about the Chesapeake Bay area, and most feature its unique cuisine.

As I worked on my first book, *The Official Crab Eater's Guide,* I spent 5 years traveling the highways and back roads around the Bay. Along the way, I'd spot a museum or an historic site I'd want to return to some day. I started compiling these gems of information, and it wasn't long before I'd collected boxes of material. That background formed the basis for this book.

Falling in love with the Chesapeake Bay is easy, especially if you know the secret hideaways. That's what this book is all about—secrets. I know the Bay as well as anyone, and I've explored its nooks and crannies. The Baytripper travel guides are your guides to a unique place. We've got what it takes to make your next trip a pleasure.

Enjoying the outdoors is a major pastime here. You'll find scenic creeks, rivers and marshes. There are a number of nature preserves including Blackwater National Wildlife Refuge in Cambridge, Maryland. Blackwater harbors over 250 bird species and is a chief wintering area for Canadian geese and ducks. It's also a haven for three endangered species: the bald eagle, Delmarva fox squirrel, and Peregrine Falcon. The 5-mile wildlife drive is a good way to explore the park. I've also listed beaches that may be new to you where you can sunbathe or build sand castles; and I've included great creeks for fishing and first-rate crabbing piers.

Local festivals regularly celebrate life by the Bay. In late October, you can cross the busiest drawbridge in the world to enjoy a special day of play at Tilghman Island. Tilghman Island Day is a tribute to the local watermen. Fresh steamed crabs are served at the firehouse, and locals can help you practice your oyster shucking. Artisans sell their wares, and area authors (often including myself) are on hand to sign their books. A highlight of the day is a cruise aboard the shipjacks, the workboats used to harvest local oysters.

Inside this guide you'll find listings for boat trips of all types, from ferry rides to charter fishing and crabbing excursions to sailing lessons or tours of city harbors. You could also cross over and under the Chesapeake Bay where it meets the Atlantic Ocean. The Chesapeake Bay Bridge Tunnel connects the Eastern Shore with Norfolk, Virginia. This multi-million dollar structure is acclaimed one of the Seven Wonders of the Modern World.

I've pointed out places to see in the special cities and towns along your tour, which begins with Chesapeake City, Maryland, and ends at Cape Charles, Virginia. As you tour, you could stop at one or all of the following places. A visit to St. Michaels, an historic port on the Miles River, is a must. A restored lighthouse is one of the major attractions at the Chesapeake Maritime Museum, along with historic bay craft such as the log canoe, one of the earliest authentic American boats. You'll want to visit Smith Island, a bay world all its own. This low-lying island boasts that 90 percent of its small population are watermen. The residents speak a local language that is a mixture of old colloquial English and modern-day Eastern Shore.

These are just a few of my favorites. Skim the pages and select your own. You're about to discover a region packed with something for everyone—just follow the water!

HOW TO USE THIS BOOK

For ease of use, *Baytripper* is divided into two volumes. Volume I, the Eastern Shore, explores the towns from Chesapeake City, Maryland, in the north to Cape Charles, Virginia, in the south. Volume II, the Western Shore, covers the region from Norfolk, Virginia, in the south, to Elkton, Maryland, in the North.

Each chapter begins with a map of the area indicating the locations of the towns that dot the roads, fields, rivers, and creeks. Introducing each town is a description painting a broad picture of the historic, geographic, economic, and other factors that contribute to it's individual character.

You can begin your circle tour of the historic Chesapeake Bay region at any point along the 800-mile route. Those living in neighboring areas might choose a town that is closest to them. Continue clockwise or counterclockwise around the circle tour, seeing something new and doing something different each mile. There is no need to backtrack. You can stay on the main highways between the attractions or you can branch off on the back roads and chart your own route to discovery. Create your own unique experience using the *Baytripper* travel guides, moving at your own pace, emphasizing the things you want to see and do.

DISCLAIMER

While every care has been taken to ensure the accuracy of the information in this guide, the passage of time will always bring change, and consequently the publisher cannot accept responsibility for errors that may occur. The prudent Baytripper will avoid inconvenience by calling ahead.

CREDIT CARDS ARE ABBREVIATED AS FOLLOWS:

AE - American Express
CB - Carte Blanche
D   - Discover Card
DC - Diner's Club
MC - Master Card
V   - Visa

UPPER BAY

Chesapeake City to Centreville

Follow the water....

- Chesapeake City
- Georgetown
- Betterton
- Rock Hall
- Chestertown
- Centreville

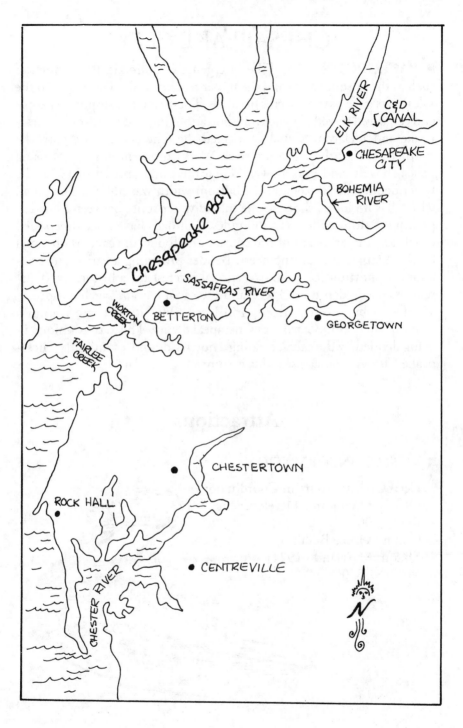

CHESAPEAKE CITY

■ **BACKGROUND:** Until the emergence of railroads, Bay tributaries such as the Susquehanna and the upper reaches of the Potomac and the Elk Rivers gave rise to systems of canals. These canals transported people and cargo and served as major transportation routes. The 13-mile Chesapeake and Delaware Canal connected the Chesapeake Bay with the northern end of the Delaware river. Work commenced in 1824 using picks, shovels, and horsepower. When the canal opened in 1929, the water depth was 10 feet and the bottom width was 36 feet. The canal, which has no locks, shortens the inland water route between Philadelphia and Baltimore by over 200 miles. Railroads have since superseded canals as a major means of transportation. Today, the canal is operated by the Army Corps of Engineers. Besides providing a variety of recreational opportunities, it holds a special interest for a historians. (Current operating depth is 33 feet, and the canal has a navigable width of 450 feet. The lowest bridge is 133 feet.) One city that grew up as a result of the C&D Canal was Chesapeake City. This city is unique in being divided by the canal, creating a north side and a south side Chesapeake City. As you can see, this is truly a canal town.

Attractions

■ **VISITOR INFORMATION**

Cecil County Tourism Coordinator
Office of Economic Development
Room 300
County Office Building
Elkton, Maryland 21921
410-996-5300

■ BOAT CHARTERS

Miss Clare Charter Fishing
Front Street
Chesapeake City, Maryland
21921
410-885-5088

Charter excursions April through October. Admission charge.

■ GUIDED SIGHTSEEING TOURS

Hill Holiday's Travel Center
103 Bohemia Avenue
Chesapeake City, Maryland
219 25
410-885-2797
800-874-4558

For the first time, the picturesque Cecil County Horse Country now offers a complete tour package. Join Hill Holiday's as they personally escort you through the illustrious history of Cecil County and show the rural splendor of the Chesapeake Bay tidal area. Discover the land that resides at "the peak of the Chesapeake." Weekends only. Fee.

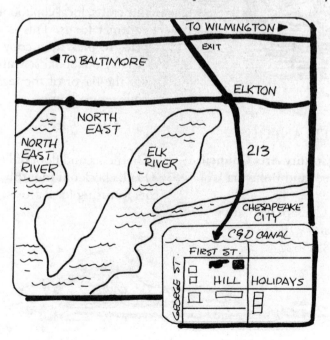

■ HISTORIC SITES

Chesapeake City Historic District
South Chesapeake City,
Maryland 21915
410-885-2795

Almost lost in the mist of the past is the name "Bohemia Village," a small collection of fishermen's cabins that once nestled along Back Creek where Chesapeake City now stands. The Irish arrived with picks and shovels in 1824 to build a canal. Where the workers settled, Chesapeake City sprang into existence. Today, a high level, arched "rainbow bridge" carries Route 213 far above the little canal town.

Baytrippers should visit such places as the Back Creek General Store at 100 Bohemia Avenue. It's beautifully restored and specializes in unusual gifts, fine crafts, local cookbooks, and gourmet foods. This is a good place to pick up a copy of my "Crab Cookbook" so you can savor the flavor of the region on your return home.

■ MISCELLANEOUS

Cecil County Arts Council
1st Street and Bohemia
Avenue
South Chesapeake City,
Maryland 21915
410-885-5622

On the second floor of Franklin Hall, check out monthly exhibits featuring local artists. Free.

■ MUSEUMS

C&D Canal Museum
2nd Street and Bethel Road
Chesapeake City, Maryland
21915
410-885-5622

The C&D Canal Museum depicts the history and operation of the Chesapeake and Delaware Canal. The old lock pumphouse is a national register site and highlights a working model of a waterwheel and lock steam engine. Also shown are paintings, maps, documents, and artifacts pertaining to the history of the waterway. Open from Easter to Thanksgiving, Monday to Saturday, 8 a.m. to 4:15 p.m.; Sunday 10 a.m. to 6 p.m. Closed major holidays and on Sundays from Thanksgiving to Easter. Free.

■ PARKS AND GARDENS

Pell Garden
South Chesapeake City,
Maryland 21915
410-885-5298

Today, the tow path that parallels the canal is used by hikers and cyclists. The canal provides pleasant opportunities for boating, fishing, and birdwatching. Be sure to stop by the observation point for the canal. Free.

■ SEASONAL EVENTS

Canal Days
Bohemia Avenue
South Chesapeake City,
Maryland 21915
410-996-5300

Canal Days are celebrated with music, artisans, carriage rides, crab feasts, and a wonderful view of the water. Last Saturday in June, 10 a.m. to 6 p.m. Free.

FOOD FOR EVERY TASTE! CRABS ★ CRAB CAKES ★ POLISH SAUSAGE ★ HOT DOGS ★ PIZZA HAMBURGERS ★ MEATBALL SANDWICHES ★ SLOPPY JOES ★ COLD DRINKS BAKED GOODS ★ POPCORN ★ CANDY ★ ROAST BEEF SANDWICHES FUNNEL CAKES ★ BARBECUED CHICKEN ★ FRENCH FRIES

Restaurants

Bayard House
11 Bohemia Avenue
South Chesapeake City, Maryland
21915
410-885-4040

Enjoy fine dining in an elegant atmosphere overlooking the canal. Open daily for lunch and dinner. Credit cards: AE, MC, and V.

Dockside Yacht Club
205 Second Street
South Chesapeake City,
Maryland 21915
410-885-5016

A splendid waterfront location that boasts of a fine restaurant specializing in fresh seafood, prime rib, and homemade veal dishes carefully prepared to your order. Open to club members from March to December. Annual membership is $1. Open for lunch and dinner. Credit cards: AE, MC, and V.

Schaefer's Canal House
Bank Street
North Chesapeake City,
Maryland 21915
410-885-2200

Schaefer's Canal House, where excellent food is served in a setting that resembles the interior of a ship. The atmosphere is casual but not unsophisticated. Large windows on three sides provide unobstructed views of the waterway and passing ships. Watch ocean-going cargo carriers as well as small, local working craft. Both are sure to provide interest. Docking is available. Open daily for lunch and dinner. Credit cards: MC, V.

The Tap Room
201 Bohemia Avenue
South Chesapeake City,
Maryland 21915
410-885-2344

This laid back, family-style restaurant features steamed crabs, seafood, and homemade Italian specialties. You'll always find a crowd in the tap room, and it's a fun place to be. Open daily for lunch and dinner.

Accommodations

You won't find big hotels or even smaller motels in Chesapeake City. You can, however, spend the night on the waterfront in a circa 1854 home where famous Jack Conner, author of the "Blue Max," once lived. Or spend a charming night at the Inn at the Canal, a lovely 1867 Victorian that is now a bed and breakfast.

■ BED AND BREAKFASTS

Blue Max
300 Bohemia Avenue
South Chesapeake City, Maryland 21915
410-885-2781

Bohemia House
1236 Town Point Road
South Chesapeake City, Maryland 21915
410-885-3024

Inn at the Canal
104 Bohemia Avenue
South Chesapeake City, Maryland 21915
410-885-5995

McNulty House at Schaefer's
208 Bank Street
North Chesapeake City, Maryland 21915
410-885-2200

GEORGETOWN

■ **BACKGROUND:** On this site in 1812, the residents of Fredericktown built Fort Duffy—one of the many forts built for the country's defense against the British. In 1813, an invading British fleet burned the fort, Fredericktown, and neighboring Georgetown. Both had been named after the sons of King George III.

Attractions

■ **VISITOR INFORMATION**

Kent County Chamber of Commerce
118 North Cross Street
Chestertown, Maryland 21620
410-778-0416

■ **HISTORIC SITES**

Kitty Knight House
Route 213
Georgetown, Maryland 21930
410-648-5777

Since Georgetown was burned to the ground by the British during the War of 1812, nothing remains except for two big, old brick houses situated on the high southern bank of the river. These beautiful, rambling, Georgian buildings were saved by a feisty woman named Kitty Knight. She refused to leave her home because she was nursing an elderly woman next door. The British officers showed mercy and left both residences standing while the rest of the abandoned town burned. Today, the two houses are merged into an inn and restaurant that overlooks Georgetown Harbor.

Mount Harmon Plantation
P.O. Box 65
Grove Neck Road
Earleville, Maryland 21919
410-275-2721

Beautifully restored 18th century tobacco plantation on the banks of the Sassafras River. Open for tours throughout the season, April through October. Admission charge.

■ HISTORIC TOWNS:

Galena, Maryland

Galena is the former site of Downs Crossroads. In 1813, pure silver, which was discovered near the town, was mined and carted to Philadelphia. The mine was closed during the War of 1812 when the owner was afraid the British would capture it. The town may have been given the name Galena because of the type of silver that was mined.

■ HUNTING

Hopkins Game Farm
Route 298
Kennedyville, Maryland
21645
410-348-5287

Hopkins Game Farm invites you to test your hunting skills on this preserve, which consists of 150 acres. There are various types of hunting, and skilled guides will take you on an outing you'll be telling your friends about for years to come. All hunts include a guide and dog. You'll be looking for pheasant, quail, and chukar. (Chukar are Old World partridges, which resemble gray partridge and were introduced into this country some time ago.) Fee.

19

■ MUSEUMS

Kent Museum
Route 448 at Turners Creek
Public Landing
Kennedyville, Maryland
21645
410-348-5721

The Kent Museum has indoor and outdoor exhibits of farm machinery dating from the last two centuries. It is a working farm, so expect to see activities such as planting and tending to fields. The museum also has a nature trail that wanders down to Turner Creek. Open from April through September. Free.

Restaurants

The Granary
Route 213
Georgetown, Maryland 21930
410-275-8177

This restaurant's specialties include crab soup, crab cakes, seafood platter, clams or oyster Rockefeller, smoked fish du jour, crab meat cocktail, and crab imperial. Open for lunch and dinner. Credit cards: AE, MC, and V.

Kitty Knight House
Route 213
Georgetown, Maryland 21930
410-648-5777

Inside the Kitty Knight House's dining room and cozy bar, the ceilings are beamed, the floors are pegged, and the walls are panelled. House specialties include cold water lobster tail and petite filet mignon with mushrooms bearnaise sauce. Or how about brook trout Cockburn—fresh brook trout stuffed with spinach, mushrooms, and blue cheese, then baked to perfection. Open for lunch and dinner. Credit cards: AE, MC, and V.

Vonnie's Restaurant
Route 213 and 298
Kennedyville, Maryland 21645
410-778-5300

Vonnie's Restaurant brings out the best in buffets. On Tuesday, it's Mexican, Wednesday, it's Italian, Thursday, feast on Chinese food. On Friday and Saturday, it's seafood and chicken and on Sunday the offering is ham and turkey. Buffets include soup, appetizer, salad, dessert and bread bar. Open daily for breakfast, lunch and dinner. Credit cards: MC and V.

Accommodations

■ **BED AND BREAKFASTS**

Kitty Knight House
Route 213, Box 97
Georgetown, Maryland 21930
410-648-5777

■ **HOTELS, MOTELS, AND INNS**

Vonnie's Motel
Route 213 and 298
Kennedyville, Maryland 21645
410-778-6412

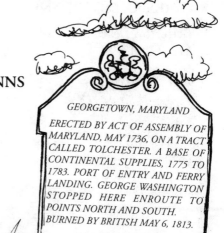

GEORGETOWN, MARYLAND

ERECTED BY ACT OF ASSEMBLY OF MARYLAND, MAY 1736, ON A TRACT CALLED TOLCHESTER. A BASE OF CONTINENTAL SUPPLIES, 1775 TO 1783. PORT OF ENTRY AND FERRY LANDING. GEORGE WASHINGTON STOPPED HERE ENROUTE TO POINTS NORTH AND SOUTH. BURNED BY BRITISH MAY 6, 1813.

Erected by
London Bridge Chapter D.A.R.
1932

BETTERTON

■ **BACKGROUND:** Betterton was originally planned as a sophisticated summer resort for affluent residents of Baltimore, Philadelphia, and Washington. It was accessible only by steamboat. In 1887, an amusement pier was built, and the town boasted of 12 hotels for accommodation of only "proper men and their proper ladies." Proper attire was required at meals as well. Betterton is located on the site of an early farm named "Fish Hall." When the first house in Betterton was torn down in the early 1900's, skulls were discovered. Historians tell us the skulls had been buried to keep ghosts away. With the coming of steamboats, Betterton developed as a resort; likewise, with the decline of the steamboat, the influx of visitors diminished. Today, it has been redeveloped as a residential resort community. It is still beautifully situated on the Sassafras River where this waterway joins with the Chesapeake Bay.

Attractions

■ **PARKS AND GARDENS**

Betterton Beach and Park
410-778-1948

Visitors can enjoy the town's sandy beach, which stretches along the Bay. It is monitored in the summer by lifeguards. A bathhouse and volleyball nets add to summer fun. Free.

■ SEASONAL EVENTS

Betterton Day
410-778-0416

A delightful, small town affair with a parade, baby contest, crab cakes, and hot dogs. Just head for the waterfront, where the Sassafras River meets the Bay. First Saturday in August, 10:30 a.m. to 5 p.m. Free.

Accommodations

■ BED AND BREAKFASTS

Lantern Inn Bed and Breakfast
115 Ericsson Avenue
Betterton, Maryland 21610
410-348-5809

■ HOTELS, MOTELS, AND INNS

Still Pond Inn
Still Pond Road
Still Pond, Maryland 21661
410-348-2234

CHESTERTOWN

■ **BACKGROUND:** Chestertown, located 21 nautical miles from the Chesapeake Bay, was founded in 1706 and became an important point of entry in colonial times. Several of the venerable homes on Water Street were built by merchants involved in foreign shipping in the 18th and 19th centuries. For over 150 years, colorful steamboats were the favorite form of transportation for passengers and freight. During the 1920s, Adam's Floating Theatre tied up at the wharf and people from all over the country traveled to Chestertown for an evening of entertainment and pleasure on the Bay. The downtown area of Chestertown includes one of the richest concentrations of handsome, 18th century buildings in the Tidewater Area. It has been designated as a national historic landmark.

Attractions

■ **VISITOR INFORMATION**

Kent County Chamber of Commerce
P.O. Box 146
118 North Cross Street
Chestertown, Maryland 21620
410-778-0416

■ **CRABBING**

Captain Clay Larrimore
305 Campus Avenue
Chestertown, Maryland 21620
410-778-0616

The fully-licensed Captain Larrimore sets a long trotline baited with bull lips (yes, bull lips!) and lets his customers take turns dipping for crabs. This summer outing is guaranteed to please, and gives you a chance to experience part of the life of a Chesapeake Bay waterman. The best part is that you get to keep the crabs you catch! Admission charge.

■ HUNTING

John F. Price III and Sons
24133 Chestertown Road
Chestertown, Maryland 21620
410-778-4655

Successful hunting in the Upper Bay is a Maryland tradition. My suggestion for a successful hunt is to begin with an experienced guide. Call Buck, John, Joey or Jimmy for your booking. Seasonal. Fee.

■ MUSEUMS

Geddes-Piper House
Church Alley
Chestertown, Maryland 21620
410-778-3499

An example of a Philadelphia townhouse with 18th century furniture and a historical library. Open May to October, Saturday and Sunday, 1 p.m. to 4 p.m. Admission charge. .

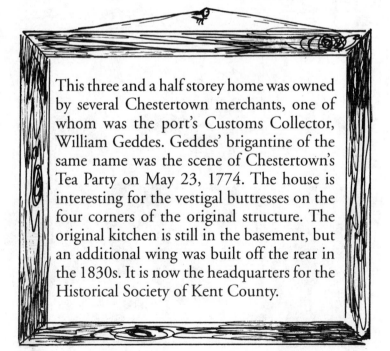

This three and a half storey home was owned by several Chestertown merchants, one of whom was the port's Customs Collector, William Geddes. Geddes' brigantine of the same name was the scene of Chestertown's Tea Party on May 23, 1774. The house is interesting for the vestigal buttresses on the four corners of the original structure. The original kitchen is still in the basement, but an additional wing was built off the rear in the 1830s. It is now the headquarters for the Historical Society of Kent County.

■ SEASONAL EVENTS

Chestertown Tea Party Festival
Main Street
Chestertown, Maryland 21620
410-778-0416

Inspired by the original Boston Tea Party, Chestertown citizens staged one of their own. On May 23, 1774, they boarded the "William Geddes," a tea-laden brigadeen anchored in the Chester River. The tea was thrown overboard. Today the annual commemoration takes place along downtown city streets and recalls the local merchants' revolt against the British tea tax. Special crafts, local foods, dulcimer music, street dancing concessions, and reenactment highlight the day. End of May. Free.

Wildlife Show
P.O. Box 146, Main Street
Chestertown, Maryland 21620
410-778-0416

The Wildlife Show of arts and crafts is held annually in Chestertown. The show is perfect for a day trip or weekend getaway. It is held on the campus of the historic Washington College on Main Street on a Saturday and Sunday in late October. Over 80 exhibitors will display their work. Many demonstrate their craft. Admission charge.

■ **TOURS**

Candlelight Walking Tour of Chestertown
P.O. Box 665
Chestertown, Maryland 21620
410-778-3499

Each year in late September, the Historical Society of Kent County asks the owners of some of the town's historic homes and buildings to open their doors for the candlelight tour. After days of preparation, the candles are lit and the doors are opened— come rain or shine. The large number of buildings may make it impossible for you to visit them all during the four-hour tour. We suggest you first select those you would most like to see and visit others as time allows. Evening of the third Saturday in September. Admission charge.

Christmas in Chestertown
P.O. Box 146
118 North Cross Street
Chestertown, Maryland 21620
410-778-0416

A tour of the interiors of period homes and buildings, all decorated in Yuletide splendor. Admission charge.

Tours, cont.

Echo Hill Outdoor School
Worton, Maryland 21678
410-348-5880
410-348-5303

Week-long trips, mainly for children. Options include canoeing, skipjack sailing, oyster buy boats, and trot-lining for blue crabs. This is a non-profit environmental school approved by the Maryland State Department of Education. Reservations required. Admission charge.

Walking Tour of Old Chestertown
118 North Cross Street
Chestertown, Maryland 21620
410-778-0416

Throughout the 18th century, Chestertown was recognized as the busiest port on Maryland's eastern shore. It became home to a number of prosperous merchants and shipowners. They built elegant homes along the river's edge now within easy walking distance of shops. Stop by the Chamber of Commerce Office, and pick up your copy of the walking tour brochure. Experience the downtown district which has made Chestertown so popular. Free.

■ MISCELLANEOUS

Remington Farms
Route 20
Chestertown, Maryland 21620
410-778-1565

Remington Farms shows how farming and wildlife management can coexist, each complimenting the other. All year 'round, you can sit in your car and observe a sanctuary pond near the office. Tens of thousands of Canada geese, mallards, pin-tails, and other types of ducks fly into the pond during seasonal migrations. From February to October, during daylight hours, you can explore the three-thousand-acre, wildlife research and demonstration area using a free brochure for a self-guided driving tour. Stop by the office for a map. Pond available for viewing year 'round. Driving tour open February to mid-October, daylight hours. Both free.

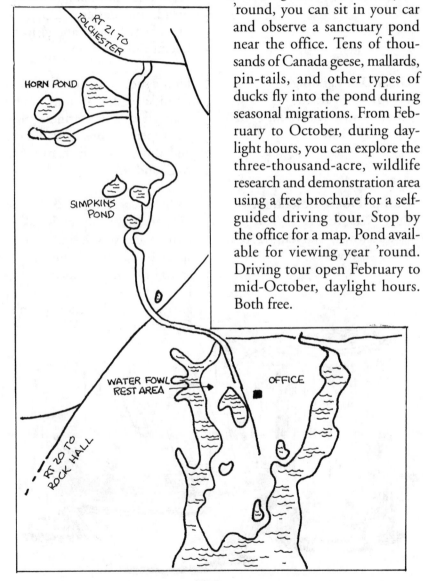

Restaurants

Buzz's Restaurant
Route 213 and 291
Chestertown, Maryland 21620
410-778-1214

Full-service restaurant specializing in fresh seafood, hand-cut beef, and Eastern Shore poultry, as well as homemade soups, bread, and desserts. Open for breakfast, lunch, and dinner. Credit cards: MC, V.

Great Oak Landing
Handy Point Road
Chestertown, Maryland 21620
410-778-2100

House specialties include filet of flounder, stuffed shrimp, jumbo crab cakes, and mariners' platter. Open for breakfast, lunch, and dinner. Credit cards: AE, MC, and V.

Harbor House Restaurant
Buck Neck Road
Chestertown, Maryland 21620
410-778-0669

Delicious seafood is served for dinner, including crab cakes, homemade soups, and nightly specials. Harbor House is located in a lovely wooded setting. It's all here—a quiet harbor, a great view, and friendly people. Credit cards: MC, V.

Imperial Hotel
208 High Street
Chestertown, Maryland 21620
410-778-5000

House specials include seafood and salads, as well as crusty rolls and desserts baked on the premises. Open for dinner only; closed Sunday and Monday. Credit cards: MC, V.

Ironstone Cafe
236 Cannon Street
Chestertown, Maryland 21620
410-778-0188

Eastern Shore-style French and Italian cooking. Open Tuesday to Saturday for lunch and dinner; closed Sunday and Monday. Credit cards: MC, V.

Old Wharf Inn
Foot of Cannon Street
Chestertown, Maryland 21620
410-778-3566

Offering Eastern Shore hospitality, fresh seafood, steaks, and chicken. Open daily for lunch and dinner. Credit cards: MC, V.

Accommodations

■ BED AND BREAKFASTS

Brampton Inn
Route 20
Chestertown, Maryland 21620
410-778-1860

Cole House B&B
Route 290
Crumpton, Maryland 21628
410-928-5287

Drop the Anchor Inn
Truslow Road
Chestertown, Maryland 21620
410-778-1004

Great Oak Manor
10568 Cliff Road
Chestertown, Maryland 21620
410-778-5796

Hill's Inn
114 Washington Avenue
Chestertown, Maryland 21620
410-778-1926

Inn at Mitchell House
8796 Maryland Parkway
Chestertown, Maryland 21620
410-778-6500

Inn at Rolph's Wharf
Rolphs Wharf Road
Chestertown, Maryland 21620
410-778-1926

Lauretum Inn
954 High Street
Chestertown, Maryland 21620
410-778-3236

White Swan Tavern
231 High Street
Chestertown, Maryland 21620
410-778-2300

Widow's Walk Inn
402 High Street
Chestertown, Maryland 21620
410-778-6455

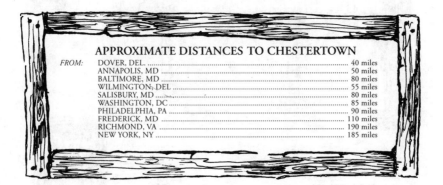

APPROXIMATE DISTANCES TO CHESTERTOWN

FROM:	
DOVER, DEL.	40 miles
ANNAPOLIS, MD	50 miles
BALTIMORE, MD	80 miles
WILMINGTON, DEL	55 miles
SALISBURY, MD	80 miles
WASHINGTON, DC	85 miles
PHILADELPHIA, PA	90 miles
FREDERICK, MD	110 miles
RICHMOND, VA	190 miles
NEW YORK, NY	185 miles

■ HOTELS, MOTELS, AND INNS

Courtyard Inn
Route 213 South
Chestertown, Maryland 21620
410-778-2755

Foxley Manor Motel
609 Washington Avenue
Chestertown, Maryland 21612
410-778-3200

Imperial Hotel
208 High Street
Chestertown, Maryland 21620
410-778-5000

ROCK HALL

■ **BACKGROUND:** Rock Hall in colonial times was a stopover point on the road to Philadelphia and New York. Travelers would cross the Bay by packet boat from Annapolis and board the stagecoach here. The stage route, taken by George Washington, ran through Chestertown and then turned north to follow what is Route 213 today. Rock Hall is known primarily for its fishing and seafood businesses. The latter supply fish, crabs, oysters, and softshell crabs direct to markets as far away as New England. Once the terminus of an auto ferry that crossed the Chesapeake Bay from Baltimore, Rock Hall has grown to be a center for the sportsman seeking game in the sky or beneath the waves. Rock Hall has two excellent harbors, just minutes from the Chesapeake Bay and many boating facilities. Some light industry prospers here along with many marine-oriented commercial activities.

Attractions

■ **VISITOR INFORMATION**

Town of Rock Hall
South Main Street
P.O. Box 8
Rock Hall, Maryland 21661
410-639-7611

■ **BOAT CHARTERS**

Daddy's Girl Charter
5681 S. Hawthorne Avenue
Rock Hall, Maryland 21661
410-778-9424

Fish the Upper Chesapeake Bay with Captain Bob Gibson. His 30 years of fishing experience will guide you to the "Big Ones". Fishing rod and tackle provided. Call for your fishing schedule. Fee.

- SPRING ROCKFISH TROPHY SEASON
- BOTTOM FISHING— (JUNE — SEPT)
  PERCH, SPOT, CATFISH & BLUEFISH
- FALL ROCKFISH SEASON

■ BOAT RENTALS

East Neck Rowboat Rentals
Eastern Neck Island
Rock Hall, Maryland 21661
410-639-7100

Try your hand at "chicken neck'n" for crabs from a row boat, or just enjoy getting out on the water. June to September. Fee.

■ HUNTING

Wayne Gatling Guide Service
25046 E. Kentfield Road
Worton, Maryland 21678
410-778-3191
800-289-0474

Waterfowl hunting with Wayne Gatling on Maryland's Eastern Shore, which is recognized by sportsmen to be the best waterfowl hunting on the Atlantic flyway. For more than 20 years Wayne has guided goose and duck hunting parties. You may choose duck hunting in the marsh, goose hunts in the corn fields or combination hunts on ponds and creeks. Seasonal. Call for your schedule. Fee.

■ MUSEUMS

Rock Hall Museum
South Main Street
Municipal Building
Rock Hall, Maryland 21661
410-778-1399

Discover Indian artifacts, nautical relics, and a replica of a vanished 18th century town. Open year 'round, Wednesday to Sunday, 2 p.m. to 4 p.m. Admission charge.

The Waterman's Museum
Route 20
Rock Hall, Maryland 21661
410-778-6697

The Chesapeake Bay Oyster has been praised for centuries and is a tradition well worth preserving. Photographs, exhibits, workboats, and tools that highlight this heritage are on display at the Waterman's Museum. Open daily 10 a.m. to 5 p.m. Free.

▪ PARKS AND GARDENS

Eastern Neck Wildlife Refuge
Route 445
Rock Hall, Maryland 21661
410-639-7056

The Chesapeake Bay watershed lies within a major north/south waterfowl migration path known as the Atlantic Flyway. Mountain chains to the west and coastal shorelines to the east channel millions of migrating birds through the Bay region. This wildlife refuge provides an excellent vantage point for viewing dramatic spring and fall migrations. Free.

WILDLIFE CALENDAR

Most waterfowl begin arriving in early October. Their numbers reach a peak in November. Tundra swan, Canada geese, bufflehead, wigeon, pintail, mallard, black duck, canvasback, and scaup are the principal waterfowl using the refuge. The presence of sea ducks such as the oldsquaw and white-winged scoter makes the refuge more interesting. Most waterfowl leave the refuge by early April. Shorebirds, wading and marsh birds such as herons, egrets and rails, frequent the shores and marshes of the refuge all year.

The diversity of habitat, including the shoal waters, sand beaches, open fields, marshes, swamps, hedgerows, and woodlands provide for a variety of bird life. Upland game birds include bobwhite and mourning doves. Bald eagles and osprey nest on the island. Various woodpeckers, along with many songbirds, can be seen in the timbered areas and hedgerows.

Restaurants

Bay Harbor Restaurant
5707 Bayside Avenue
Rock Hall, Maryland 21661
410-639-7177

At Bay Harbor Restaurant you will enjoy fresh seafood with a scenic view of the Rock Hall Harbor. My favorite is the broiled seafood combo. Open daily for lunch and dinner. Credit cards: MC, V.

Fin, Fur, and Feather
20895 Bayside Avenue
Rock Hall, Maryland 21661
410-639-7454

Rock Hall is beautiful throughout the year, but many people say their favorite time to visit here is in the fall when geese, ducks, and swans darken the sunset sky. The menu at the Fin, Fur, and Feather will also delight you. House specialties include fisherman's chowder, crab soup, clam chowder, oyster stew, steamed oysters, stuffed shrimp, fried clam strips, soft shell crabs, broiled oysters, and fish of the day. Open for breakfast, lunch, and dinner; closed from 3 p.m. to 5 p.m.

Old Oars Inn
Main Street
Rock Hall, Maryland 21661
410-639-2541

The Inn at Osprey
20786 Rock Hall Avenue
Rock Hall, Maryland 21661
410-639-2194

Local seafood, sandwiches, pizza, and friendly atmosphere in the heart of downtown Rock Hall. Open daily for lunch and dinner.

What do you get when you combine a touch of Ireland, the feel of Williamsburg, and a taste of the Bay? You get the Inn at the Osprey. Located in the seclusion of the Haven on Swan Creek. Open Thursday through Sunday, dinner only. Credit Cards: MC, V.

Restaurants, cont.

Waterman's Crab House
Sharp Street Wharf
Rock Hall, Maryland 21661
410-639-2261

Rock Hall is a working harbor. In winter, you'll find warmth in eating the local oyster stews and chowders. In summer, treat yourself to a frosty mug of beer and a dozen steamed crabs while enjoying views of the Rock Hall Harbor from the restaurant's back porch. Waterman's is open for lunch and dinner daily. Credit cards: MC, V.

Accommodations

■ BED AND BREAKFASTS

Black Duck Inn
21096 Chesapeake Avenue
Rock Hall, Maryland 21661
410-639-2478

Moonlight Bay
6002 Lawton Avenue
Rock Hall, Maryland 21661
410-639-2660

Huntingfield Manor
Route 445
Chestertown, Maryland 21620
410-778-1327

Napley Green Country Inn
Route 445
Rock Hall, Maryland 21661
410-639-2267

■ CAMPING

Ellendale Campsites
Route 445
Rock Hall, Maryland 21661
410-639-7485

■ HOTELS, MOTELS, AND INNS

Mariners Motel
33 South Hawthorne Avenue
Rock Hall, Maryland 21661
410-639-2291

Osprey Point Inn
20876 Rock Hall Avenue
Rock Hall, Maryland 21661
410-639-2194

Swan Point Inn
Route 20 and Coleman Road
Rock Hall, Maryland 21661
410-639-2500

CENTREVILLE

■ **BACKGROUND:** With understated hospitality and subtle elegance, Centreville welcomes all Baytrippers. Named for its central and easily accessible location, Centreville became an incorporated town in 1794. It was chartered as the seat of Queen Anne's County, where a statue of the county's namesake graces the courthouse green. The courthouse itself symbolizes the close ties that Centreville retains with its past. The building is the oldest Maryland courthouse; it has been in continuous use since 1792.

Attractions

■ **VISITOR INFORMATION**

Centreville Town Hall
101 Lawyers Road
Centreville, Maryland 21617
410-758-1180

Queen Anne's County Chamber of Commerce
P.O. Box 496
Chester, Maryland 21619
410-758-2300

■ **HISTORIC SITES**

Queen Anne's County Courthouse and Statue of Queen Anne
122 North Commerce Street
Centreville, Maryland 21619
410-758-0322

One of two 18th century courthouses in Maryland used continuously since 1792. The bronze statue of Queen Anne was dedicated by today's Princess Anne of Great Britain.

Tucker House
124 South Commerce Street
Centreville, Maryland 21617
410-758-1494

Built in 1794, this is the Queen Anne's Historical Society's oldest house in Centreville with period furnishings and memorabilia. Open by appointment only. Free.

Wright's Chance
119 South Commerce Street
Centreville, Maryland 21617
410-758-1494

Queen Anne's Historical Society's early plantation house, noted for original wood paneling. Excellent collection of early American Queen Anne furniture. Open by appointment only. Free.

Restaurants

Hillside Inn Crab House
Route 213
Centreville, Maryland 21617
410-758-1300
410-758-2707

Cuisine features steaks, and steamed and fried seafood. Open for breakfast, lunch, and dinner. Credit cards: AE, MC, and V.

Accommodations

■ BED AND BREAKFASTS

Corsica Wharf Inn
Route 304
Creamery Lane
Centreville, Maryland 21617
410-758-3950

The Wharf Lodge
Watson Road
Centreville, Maryland 21617
410-758-1111

Kendall House
Watson Road
Route 2, Box 58
Centreville, Maryland 21617
410-758-0159

■ HOTELS, MOTELS, AND INNS

Hillside Motel
Route 213
Centreville, Maryland 21617
410-758-2270

KENT ISLAND
Stevensville to Oxford

Follow the water....

- Stevensville
- Grasonville
- Easton
- St. Michaels
- Tilghman Island
- Oxford

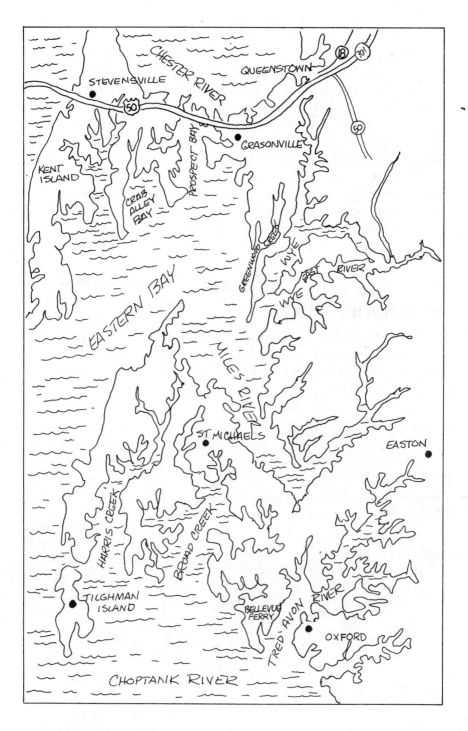

STEVENSVILLE

■ **BACKGROUND:** In 1629, William Claiborne negotiated trading rights for the British crown with Kent Island's aboriginal peoples. In 1631, the island was declared a colonial settlement under patent from King Charles I (1625-1645) of Great Britain and Ireland. The island provided Claiborne with a trading post centered between native villages in the Upper Bay and the Jamestown settlement. The island was rich in fur-bearing animals, tillable land, oysters, crabs, wild ducks, and gentle navigable coves and creeks. Today, Claiborne's "Isle of Kent" still harbors shipbuilders, farmers, and carpenters—workers who were so vital to the colonies. To many travellers, Kent Island is also the gateway to the Eastern Shore and the terminus for the Chesapeake Bay Bridge.

Attractions

■ **VISITOR INFORMATION**

Queen Anne's County Visitor's Service
1300 Main Street
Grasonville, Maryland 21638
410-827-4810

Kent Island Heritage Society
P.O. Box 321
Stevensville, Maryland 21666
410-643-5969

■ **AIRPORT**

Bay Bridge Airport
Route 3, P.O. Box 71
Stevensville, Maryland 21666
410-643-9802

Records show that Claiborne built a fort. a church, dwellings and boats. He brought the first white woman to Maryland "a mayde servant to wash our linnen, Joane Young". He laid out gardens and orchards, stocked the farms with cattle and planted 2000 tobacco plants, starting Maryland's famous tobacco economy which dominated much of colonial life. His pinnace the Long Tayle, was the first boat built in Maryland.

■ BOAT RENTALS

Crab Alley Marina
Route 1, P.O. Box 286
Chester, Maryland 21619
410-643-5588

Where else but on crab alley would you want to run a trotline or chicken neck for crabs? It'll be a fun way to spend the day. Fee.

■ CRABBING/FISHING

Romancoke Pier
Route 8
Stevensville, Maryland 21666
410-758-0835

A 1.5 acre site located at the end of Route 8 on Kent Island. It features a fishing and crabbing pier with a picnic area. The pier is open during the warm-weather months daily from 6 a.m. to 9 p.m. Out-of-county residents charged for pier use. County residents admitted free.

■ HISTORIC SITES

Cray House
Cockey's Lane
Stevensville, Maryland 21666
410-827-4810

This 185-year-old house was deeded to the Kent Island Heritage Society by the Cray heirs. The oldest part of the house has an unusual and unique construction of post and plank, 3-inch, horizontally planked walls, pegged into slotted posts. Its small size and unchanged simplicity add interest. The Cray house is listed on the National Historic Register. Open by appointment from May through October, Saturdays only, 1 p.m. to 4 p.m.

■ HISTORIC TOWNS

Stevensville Towne
Stevensville, Maryland 21666

This entire town has been placed on the National Register of Historical Sites. In addition to the Cray House and the beautiful Christ Episcopal Church, there are 17 historical structures which were built between 1840 and 1915. Pause awhile and savor the nostalgia of this small town. Store buildings date from 1870, the justice of the peace and post office from the early 20th century, and the bank from 1909.

■ PARKS AND GARDENS

Matapeake State Park
Route 8
Stevensville, Maryland 21666
410-974-1249

Matapeake State Park features an exceptionally long pier jutting out over the Bay. It offers excellent views of the Bay Bridge. Open for seasonal crabbing, fishing, and picnicking. Free.

Tuckahoe State Park
Route 50, Box 23
Queen Anne, Maryland 21657
410-634-2810

The park contains the Adkin's Arboretum, which encompasses 500 acres of wooded and floral beauty. The trees and shrubs indigenous to the state of Maryland may be viewed from meandering trails. Open daily 9 a.m. to 4 p.m. Free.

■ SEASONAL EVENTS

Kent Island Days
American Legion Hall
Stevensville, Maryland 21666
410-693-5596

Kent Island Days is an historical celebration. The activities at the hall are but just one attraction of day-long festivities spread across the island. Enjoy arts and crafts, food and drink. Perhaps the best souvenir of the island is a belly-full of crabs. Held in early May. Free.

Tuckahoe Steam and Gas Show
Route 50, P.O. Box 23
Queen Anne, Maryland 21657
410-634-2810

The annual Tuckahoe Steam and Gas Show will be located on Route 50, 5 miles north of Easton, to honor the days when steam was king. There will be 20 or more large steam engines in action providing power for sawmilling, wheat thrashing, and other operations. Also included are many old gas engines that power all types of equipment from water pumps to a saw mill. Held in mid July, Saturday and Sunday. Admission charge.

Waterman's Festival
Wells Cove
Grasonville, Maryland 21638
410-827-4810

The Queen Anne's County Waterman's Festival highlights the area's seafood heritage with annual event. Held at Kent Narrows South. Contest includes boat docking, anchor throwing, small boat rowing, crab cake contest. Sample local seafood and a pit beef. Music by "Bird Dog and the Road Kings." Held in early June, 11 a.m. to 6 p.m. Admission charge.

■ TOURS

Kent Air, Inc.
2521 Riva Road
Annapolis, Maryland 21401
410-224-0497
410-591-1360

One way to see Kent Island is through the eyes of an osprey. You will first notice that the island is 20 miles long and about 3 miles wide at its widest point. An outstanding feature is the myriad of creeks that feed the Bay. Here's your opportunity to use regional air charters for sightseeing from the Bay Bridge Airport. Call Anthony Drummond. Fee.

Restaurants

Hemingway's Restaurant
Pier One Marina
Stevensville, Maryland 21666
410-643-CRAB

This is one of the most impressive restaurant settings on the Chesapeake Bay. It's located at the foot of the eastern terminus of the Bay Bridge. The food is imaginatively prepared and beautifully served. Open daily for lunch and dinner. Credit cards: AE, MC, and V.

Kent Manor Inn
500 Kent Manor Drive
Stevensville, Maryland 21666
410-643-5757

Kent Manor Inn presents dining in a grand estate. You'll find dining rooms decorated in flattering hues of old rose, featuring high ceilings and marble mantels. Specials of the day can be preparations of crab, lobster tail, flounder, stuffed crab imperial, prime rib, and filet mignon. Specials of the evening also include sauteed soft crabs, red snapper Cajun style, and broiled scallops in herb butter. Open daily for lunch and dinner. Credit cards: AE, MC, and V.

**Kentmorr Restaurant &
Crab House**
Kentmorr Road
Stevensville, Maryland 21666
410-643-2263

Fly, motor or sail to this Maryland-style crab house. House specialties include crabcakes, crab imperial, soft crab platter, steamed crabs, B-B-Q'd shrimp, baby back ribs, crab soup, cream of crab soup, soft shell clams, cherrystone clams, crab balls and plenty of cold beer. Open daily for lunch and dinner. Credit cards: AE, D, MC, and V.

Accommodations

■ HOTELS, MOTELS, AND INNS

Kent Manor Inn
500 Kent Manor Drive
Stevensville, Maryland 21666
410-643-5757

GRASONVILLE

■ **BACKGROUND:** William Grason was the inspiration for this community's name. Grason was a county native who served as Maryland's governor from 1839 to 1842. Previous names of the town were Ford's Store and Winchester.

Attractions

■ **VISITOR INFORMATION**

Queen Anne's County Visitor's Service
1300 Main Street
Grasonville, Maryland 21638
410-827-4810

■ **BOAT RENTALS**

Schnaitman's Boat Rentals
Wye Landing Lane
P.O. Box 116
Wye Mills, Maryland 21679
410-827-7663

Wye River crabs are alleged to be the biggest crabs found around the Chesapeake Bay. Try your hand at crabbing on the Wye River in rowboats from Schnaitman's. Open at sunrise. Fee.

■ **HISTORIC TOWNS**

Queenstown
Queen Anne's County
Courthouse
Route 18
Queenstown, Maryland 21658
410-827-4810

The first county seat of Queen Anne's County, Queenstown was an 18th century shipping port of such importance that the British launched a land and sea attack on the town during the War of 1812. The brick section of the courthouse was built in 1707. The middle, wood-framed section was built in the early 1800s. Public hangings took place in Gallows Field, behind the courthouse. Tours by appointment. Free.

■ MISCELLANEOUS

Wye Grist Mill
Route 662
Wye Mills, Maryland 21679
410-827-6909

The Wye Grist Mill was built in 1671. Part of Maryland's architectural heritage, it has been restored as a working grist mill. You'll find demonstrations and "hands-on" milling, grinding, and weaving exhibits. Open to the public April 6 through December 1, Saturday and Sunday, 11 a.m. to 4 p.m.; or by appointment. Donation.

■ PARKS AND GARDENS

Horsehead Wetlands Center
Discovery Lane
Grasonville, Maryland 21638
410-827-6694

Surrounded by more than 300 acres of natural beauty, the Waterfowl Trust of North America invites you to "take a walk on the wild side." Visitor activities revolve around the new wildfowl discovery center. A fascinating and colorful flock of waterfowl, ducks, geese, and swans, from throughout North America can be observed, photographed, and enjoyed close up. When you venture outside this area and onto the trails, you become an observer of a beautiful wetlands setting. The center abounds with deer, red fox, river otter, wood ducks, Canada geese, and bald eagles. Special screenings allow you to quietly enter blinds for observing wildlife without disturbing it. Open Wednesday through Sunday, from 9 a.m. to 5 p.m.; closed major holidays. Admission charge.

Parks and Gardens, cont.

Wye Oak State Park
P.O. Box 277
Wye Mills, Maryland 21679
410-974-3771

The Wye Oak is the official state tree of Maryland; it is the symbol of the Eastern Shore. The park's Wye Oak tree is the largest white oak in Maryland, and it is believed to be one of the largest in the United States. Its height is 95 feet and the horizontal spread reaches 165 feet. The trunk is more than 25 feet in circumference. The tree is estimated to be over 450 years old. The Wye Oak is owned by the state and is in what is now a one tree state park. Free.

Restaurants

Eastern Shore hospitality is a time-honored tradition featuring crabs, corn, cantaloupe, oysters and fresh fish. One of the joys of the Eastern Shore is its incredible view of the coast line and this wonderful cuisine.

Anglers Inn
Route 18
Grasonville, Maryland 21638
410-827-6717

House specialties include softcrab sandwich, steamed crab, seafood platter, crab cake, fried shrimp, oyster stew, crab soup. and clam chowder. Open daily for breakfast, lunch. and dinner.

Annie's Paramount Steak and Seafood House
Kent Narrows Way
Grasonville, Maryland 21638
410-827-7103

At Annie's you'll dine overlooking the Chester River and Kent Narrows. That means a double treat for you: a wide variety of fresh seafood and a constant parade of boats cruising in and out of the harbor. A special feature is the cutting of all the steaks on premise which allows the Katinas Family full control over their selections. open daily for lunch and dinner. Credit cards: MC, V.

Fisherman's Inn
Route 50 at Kent Narrows
Grasonville, Maryland 21658
410-827-8807

Eastern Shore hospitality, great seafood, great steaks, and a newly opened outdoor crab deck. Open daily for lunch and dinner. Credit cards: AE, C, MC, and V.

Restaurants, cont.

Harris Crab House
Kent Narrows Way
Grasonville, Maryland 21638
410-827-8104, 410-827-9500

Harris Crab House is located on the site of departed seafood packing houses that once lined the Narrows. Popcorn shrimp and crunchy crab nuggets are popular on the two-level, outside wrap-around deck. Open daily for lunch and dinner. Credit cards MC, V.

Holly's Restaurant
Route 50 and Jackson Creek Rd.
Grasonville, Maryland 21638
410-827-8711

Come early if you come to the Eastern Shore. That way, there should be no wait for Holly's excellent Bay breakfast of home fries and coffee. Other specials include steaks, seafood, and chicken. Open daily for breakfast, lunch, and dinner.

The Narrows
Route 50
Grasonville, Maryland 21638
410-827-8113

House specialties include crab soup, crab cakes, crab imperial, soft shell crabs, soft shell clams, breaded oysters, shrimp scampi, and fish of the day. Stunning sunsets and fresh breezes grace The Narrows restaurant. Overlooking Kent Narrows and "resting on 'erster' shells, pilings, and concrete," The Narrows offers the Eastern Shore's unique sights and sounds to each of its guests. Open daily for lunch and dinner. Credit cards: CB, DC, MC, and V.

■ HOTELS, MOTELS, AND INNS

Friendship Motel
Route 1, P.O. Box 145
Grasonville, Maryland 21638
410-827-7272

Holly's
Route 50 and Jackson Creek Road
P.O. Box 507
Grasonville, Maryland 21638
410-827-8711

Comfort Inn
Route 50
Grasonville, Maryland 21638
800-228-5150

Winchester Cove Motel and Lodge
Route 50
Grasonville, Maryland 21638
410-827-8911

Sleep Inn Motel
Route 50 and VFW Road
Grasonville, Maryland 21638
410-827-8921

Accommodations

Genial Bed and Breakfast
204 Sportsman Neck Road
Queenstown, Maryland 21658
410-827-9026

EASTON

■ **BACKGROUND:** The Maryland Assembly officially named Easton in 1788, after a street plan was completed with 118 plots for houses and business. This makes Easton one of America's first "planned communities." The present courthouse was built in 1789. Following the War of 1812, many locals dropped their guns and hitched up plows, making Easton an agricultural mainstay of the region. After the Chesapeake Bay Bridge was completed, the town was engulfed by new vitality and growth. The results are fascinating; an interesting and charming town, a delightful destination, year 'round.

Attractions

■ **VISITOR INFORMATION**

Easton Chamber of Commerce
805 Goldsborough Street
Easton, Maryland 21601
410-822-4606

Historical Society of Talbot County
P.O. Box 964
Easton, Maryland 21601
410-822-0773

■ **AIRPORT**

Easton Municipal Airport
1 Airport Circle
Easton, Maryland 21601
410-822-8560

■ GUIDED SIGHTSEEING TOURS

Chesapeake Country Tours
29110 Airport Road
Easton, Maryland 21601
410-822-8225

Chesapeake Country Tours offer a variety of attractions, from antiquing and boating to museums and shopping. Each tour is personally planned to include the landmarks, sites and special interests of the person or group making the visit. Fee.

■ HISTORIC SITES

Caroline County Courthouse
Market Street
Denton, Maryland 21629
410-479-0660

After moving the county government around to seven different sites, Caroline County finally settled its county seat in Denton in 1895. A beautiful Victorian building occupies the back part of the existing structure, and includes a lovely belltower. The Colonial Revival front section of the building was built in 1966. Open Monday to Friday, 8:30 a.m. to 4:30 p.m. Free.

Third Haven Friends Meeting House
S. Washington Street
Easton, Maryland 21601
410-822-0293
Attention: Sam Webster, Caretaker

Believed to be the oldest American frame building dedicated to religious meetings, this Quaker meeting house was constructed around 1682. The town of Easton was built around this site. Visitors are welcome Monday to Saturday, 9 a.m. to 5 p.m.; Sunday meetings are held at 10 a.m. Free.

■ HUNTING

The Caroline County Shooting Preserve
T. R. Swann and Sons, Inc.
Route 3, P.O. 92
Denton, Maryland 21629
410-479-0640, 410-479-2364

Caroline County Shooting Preserve is a family-owned-and-operated hunting paradise established in 1963. They are the oldest upland game, regulated shooting area in the Mid-Shore. All hunts include dog and guide. Guided hunts for quail, pheasant, chukar, Hungarian partridge, and mallard ducks. If you miss on the hunt, you can always try the target shooting course on the premises. October through March. No Sunday hunting in Maryland. Fee.

Sea Duck Hunting
8834 Black Dog Alley
Easton, Maryland 21601
410-820-7562
410-822-0413

Call Captain Rennie Gay to book a hunt. He guarantees a fast and exciting shoot. Fee.

■ MUSEUMS

Caroline County Historical Museum and 19th Century Colonial Log Cabin Kitchen
Sunset Avenue
Greensboro, Maryland 21639
410-482-6975

The county museum contains local memorabilia. A one-room log cabin kitchen was moved to the site from Delaware, and contains domestic material from the mid-1800s. Open by appointment only. Free.

Historical Society of Talbot County
25 South Washington Street
Easton, Maryland 21601
410-822-0773

Explore history in eight buildings gathered on one block of land. Preserved houses will take you back to the 1670 Quaker "Ending of Controversie House" and to two cabinetmaker's houses, built in 1795 and 1810. Docent-guided tours may be arranged for groups. The museum also features changing historical and cultural exhibits. Museum shop and historic houses are open Tuesday through Saturday, 10 a.m. to 4 p.m.; Sunday, 1 p.m. to 4p.m. Closed Sundays from January through March. Admission charge.

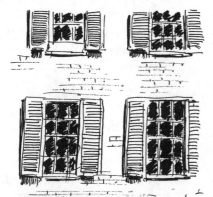

■ PARKS AND GARDENS

Martinak State Park
Deep Shore Road
Route 404, P.O. Box 12
Denton, Maryland 21629
410-479-1619

At the confluence of the Choptank River and Watt's Creek, six miles up-river from Garney's Wharf and 1 1/2 miles down-river from Denton. Hunting, fishing, bike riding, hiking, and a nature center are easily available. Free.

Pickering Creek
Environmental Center
27370 Sharp Road
Easton, Maryland 21601
410-822-4903

Pickering Creek Environmental Center is a sanctuary dedicated to community-based natural resource conservation, education and outreach on the Eastern Shore of the Chesapeake Bay. Baytrippers can walk the nature trails or enjoy one mile of shoreline on a protected tidal wetlands. Open daily 8 a.m. to 5 p.m. Free.

■ SEASONAL EVENTS

Old St. Joseph's Jousting Tournament
30300 Chapel Station Drive
Cordova, Maryland 21625
410-822-6915

Held on the grounds of Old St. Joseph's Church. Festivities include a horse show in the morning, country cookin' midday, and a jousting tournament after lunch. Held in early August. Free.

Waterfowl Festival
Downtown
Easton, Maryland 21601
410-822-4567
410-822-0773

Every fall, soon after the geese, ducks, and swans arrive to blanket the cornfields and creeks of Maryland's Eastern Shore, the town of Easton attracts its own annual migration. A three-day waterfowl festival takes over the entire town. The world's best wildlife artists, woodcarvers, and sculptors gather to command this yearly event. Throughout the festival, auctioneers bark away, selling antique and contemporary decoys. Other noisy events include the world championship goose-calling contest and Mason-Dixon regional duck-calling contest. Various other events take place around the town. Free shuttle buses carry the visitors to and from the festival. Held late November. Admission charge.

Restaurants

Cafe 25
25 Goldsborough Street
Easton, MD 21601
410-822-9360

Pat and Tom Pinto welcome you to stop in for a great Eastern Shore breakfast or lunch. It's down-home and delightful. Daily specials like the blackbean soup with steaming rice and sour cream and onion or the bread pudding with whiskey sauce make Baytrippers return for more. Open daily for breakfast, lunch, and dinner. Credit cards: MC, V.

Restaurants, cont.

Legal Spirits Pub
42 East Dover Street
(at the Avalon)
Easton, Maryland 21601
410-822-5522

Legal Spirits is the corner pub on the first floor of the Avalon Theatre. It features a full-menu restaurant and bar decorated in a prohibition theme. Specialties include burgers, crab cakes, salads, and Mexican fare. Open for lunch and dinner. Credit cards: AE, MC, and V.

Tidewater Inn
Dover and Harrison Streets
Easton, Maryland 21601
410-822-1300

The Tidewater Inn is the place to eat when visiting Easton, whether for fine dining in the Crystal Room or casual dining in the Hunter's Tavern. You will enjoy everything from the finest Eastern Shore delicacies (such as Maryland crab melt and snapper soup) to New York-style deli delights here. Open for breakfast, lunch, and dinner. Credit cards: AE, DC, MC, and V.

The Washington Street Pub
20 North Washington Street
Easton, Maryland 21601
410-822-9011

The Washington Street Pub is a true raw bar. Featured are twelve brands of COLD draft beer on tap. Your selection arrives topped with foam in a heavy mug to accompany your freshly shucked oysters and clams. Open for lunch and dinner. Credit cards: MC and V.

Accommodations

■ **BED AND BREAKFASTS**

Bishop's House
214 Goldsborough Street
Easton, Maryland 21601
410-820-7290

John S. McDaniel House
14 North Aurora Street
Easton, Maryland 21601
410-822-3704

■ **CAMPING**

Camp Mardela
Deep Short Road
Denton, Maryland 21629
410-479-2861, 410-479-3565

■ **HOTELS, MOTELS, AND INNS**

Atlantic Budget Inn
103 South Route 50
Easton, Maryland 21601
410-822-2200

Choptank Inn
North Route 50
Easton, Maryland 21601
410-822-9719

Comfort Inn
North Route 50
P.O. Box 310
Easton, Maryland 21601
410-820-8333

Econo Lodge
Route 50
Easton, Maryland 21601
410-822-6330

Mariner Motor Lodge
Route 50
Easton, Maryland 21601
410-822-4600

Tidewater Inn
Harrison and Dover Streets
Easton, Maryland 21601
410-822-130

ST. MICHAELS

■ **BACKGROUND:** Trading with the indigenous people on the Miles River began in the early 1600s. By the time Americans claimed their independence from the British, St. Michaels had gained a stronghold in the shipbuilding industry. In the early 1800s, St. Michaels was famous for building the Baltimore clipper, the sleekest sailing vessel of its time. St. Michaels became known as "the town that fooled the British" from a trick its citizens pulled while under attack. The British intended to destroy all of the shipyards around the Bay; St. Michaels was, of course, a tactical focal point. However, when the British sailed into port one night, the townsfolk had been given advance warning. They hung lanterns high in the tallest trees. Consequently, when the British fired at the only visible lights, they overshot the town. The perfect blend of historic charm and fine restaurants, shops, and the Chesapeake Bay Maritime Museum make St. Michaels truly a visitor's paradise.

Attractions

■ **VISITORS INFORMATION**

Talbot County Chamber of Commerce
805 Goldsborough Street
Easton, Maryland 21601
410-822-4606

■ **BOAT CRUISES**

Chesapeake Bay Nature Cruises and Expeditions
P.O. Box 833
St. Michaels, Maryland 21663
410-745-3255

Well-known marine biologists, Robert and Alice Lippson, will guide you aboard the Odyssey. Spend the day exploring the waterways that make up the Chesapeake Bay. The Odyssey is a custom-built, U.S. Coast Guard-certified vessel. Full, half-day, and overnight cruises are available from May through October. Admission charge.

Oxford-Bellevue Ferry
Route 329
Royal Oak, Maryland 21662
410-745-9023

This vessel is believed to be the oldest, privately owned ferry in the United States. It carries up to 10 cars and some passengers arriving by foot. You will be dropped off in Oxford after enjoying a 20-minute scenic passage across the Tred Avon River. Open May to Labor Day, Monday through Friday, 7 a.m. to 9 p.m.; and Saturday and Sunday, 9 a.m. to 9 p.m. From Labor Day to April, open Monday through Friday, 7 a.m. to sunset, and Saturday and Sunday, 9 a.m. to sunset. Closed Christmas through February. Toll.

Patriot Cruises, Inc.
P.O. Box 1206
St. Michaels, Maryland 21663
410-745-3100

The St. Michaels Patriot Cruises have plied the Miles River for over 20 years. You will appreciate Bay oysters even more after watching watermen tonging for oysters. You'll also enjoy sights —and distinctive honking—of waterfowl such as Canada geese on the Miles. All of this is viewed from the heated comfort of a 65-foot motoryacht. Weekend cruises launched at 11 a.m., 1 p.m., and 3 p.m. Admission charge.

■ CRABBING

Chicken-neckin' on the Chesapeake is a sure-fire way to experience the essence of Eastern Shore living. The St. Michaels area abounds in crabbing piers.

Sherwood Wharf
Sherwood Road
St. Michaels, Maryland 21663
410-822-2995

Harris Creek is not only a scenic beauty spot, but a great place to dangle chicken necks. It's an excellent pier for docking and crabbing. Give it a try; you'll enjoy it. Free.

Whittman Landing
Wharf Road
St. Michaels, Maryland 21663
410-822-2955

Boat launch ramp and pier for crabbing. Free.

■ HUNTING

Captain Alan T. Poore
Talbot Street
St. Michaels, Maryland 21663
410-745-3126

Very seldom do we get to turn back the hands of the clock and enjoy the good ole' days. However, hunting sea ducks on the Chesapeake Bay can recall the excitement our grandfathers enjoyed a century ago. Morning and afternoon parties are available from mid-October to mid-January. Fee.

■ MUSEUMS

Chesapeake Bay Maritime Museum
Navy Point
P.O. Box 636
St. Michaels, Maryland 21663
410-745-2916

The Chesapeake Bay Maritime Museum, located in the harbor of historic and picturesque St. Michaels, is dedicated to preserving the Bay's maritime history. Displays at the museum include the 100-year-old "Screwpile" Hooper Strait Lighthouse, a working boat-shop, comprehensive decoy exhibits, and a waterfowl taxidermy exhibit. Also of note is the Edna E. Lockwood, a restored log-bottom bugeye; a skipjack; a racing canoe; and a significant collection of Bay small craft. Open daily, 10 a.m. to 5 p.m. in the summer. Open daily, 10a.m. to 4 p.m. part of the winter but Saturday and Sunday only from January through March. Admission charge.

Museum of Costume
400 St. Mary's Square
St. Michaels, Maryland 21663
410-745-5154

Exhibits feature historic fashions reflecting early lifestyles. Open daily April through November, from noon to 5 p.m. Closed Monday. Free.

St. Mary's Square Museum
"The Green"
206 St. Mary's Square
St. Michaels, Maryland 21663
410-745-9561

The St. Mary's Square Museum, located on the town green, features local memorabilia. The Early American House contains exhibits of historic and local interest. Open May through October from 10 a.m. to 5 p.m.; or by appointment. Free.

■ SEASONAL EVENTS

Christmas in St. Michaels
Box 873
St. Michaels, Maryland 21663
410-745-3710

This weekend-long celebration is a tour of seasonally decorated homes of St. Michaels. It begins with breakfast with Santa, followed by a parade, Christmas caroling, concerts, and galleries. This event is held in various locations throughout town. Admission charge.

Crab Day
Chesapeake Bay Maritime
Museum
Navy Point
St. Michaels, Maryland 21663
410-745-2916

Crab Day celebrates the most famous Maryland crustacean—with crab races, crab picking, crab eating, exhibits, demonstrations, and plenty of good crabs. Pick up a copy of the FLAVOR OF THE CHESAPEAKE BAY COOKBOOK in the Museum gift shop. Held in early August. Admission charge.

Lighted Boat Parade
St. Michaels Harbor
St. Michaels, Maryland 21663
410-745-3531

The town of St. Michaels hosts an annual parade of lighted boats—sail boats, power boats, and work boats cruise around the harbor of this Eastern Shoretown. St. Michaels' Christmas celebration is held in mid-December. Free.

Oyster Day
Navy Point
St. Michaels, Maryland 21663
410-745-2916

Oyster Day, an annual celebration of the bivalve, is held at the Chesapeake Bay Maritime Museum. A full day of events is planned around the Chesapeake Bay oyster. The Maryland Watermen's Association puts on a cooking demonstration; watermen pass on their knowledge of oystering. Try hands-on oyster tonging and nipping demonstrations. Take a boat ride. Sample succulent fare and celebrate with musical entertainment. Held in early November. Admission charge.

Restaurants

Carpenter Street Saloon
Talbot Street, Route 33
St. Michaels, Maryland 21663
410-745-5111

You will find the locals watering down at the Carpenter Street Saloon. It features the coldest draft beer in town. The menu includes chili, hot dogs—traditional barroom fare. It's a fun place to be when in St. Michaels by the sea. Open daily for breakfast, lunch, and dinner. Credit cards: MC and V.

71

Restaurants, cont.

The Crab Claw Restaurant
Navy Point
St. Michaels, Maryland 21663
410-745-2900

The Crab Claw is located opposite the Chesapeake Bay Maritime Museum. Seize a wooden mallet and a paring knife, and let the feast begin. First, announced by their spicy aroma, come Chesapeake blue crabs steamed to a rich red. Next, roasted oysters, silky and tender. Quaff an icy beer as a taste partner to these salty treats from the Bay. Unforgettable! Open for lunch and dinner.

Lighthouse Restaurant
101 North Harbour Road
St. Michaels, Maryland 21663
410-745-9001

The Lighthouse Restaurant is part of St. Michaels Harbor, Inn, and Marina. The name stems from its location—right across the water from the lighthouse of the Chesapeake Bay Maritime Museum. The restaurant sits on the second floor, and is enclosed in glass. It provides a stupendous view of the harbor. House specialties include crab cakes, stuffed shrimp, catch of the day, shrimp scampi, soft shell crab platter, crab imperial, baked flounder, and baked stuffed flounder. Open daily for breakfast, lunch, and dinner. Credit cards: MC and V.

Town Dock Restaurant
125 Mulberry Street
St. Michaels, Maryland 21663
410-745-5577

Tiny St. Michaels, with its big history, picturesque tree-lined streets, comfortable homes, and narrow brick walkways, invites Baytrippers to a relaxed, unhurried setting. A good way to take in the incredible view of the harbor is with a meal at the Town Dock, which specializes in fresh seafood prepared with Eastern Shore flair and flavor. Open daily for lunch and dinner. Credit cards: AE, MC, and V.

Higgin's Crab House
Route 33
St. Michaels, Maryland 21663
410-745-5056

Higgin's Crab House, as you can tell by its name, is a seafood-oriented restaurant, with a full-service menu that includes such specialties as oysters on the half shell, fresh local rock fish, and various daily dinner specials. Open daily for lunch and dinner. Credit cards: MC and V.

St. Michaels Crab House
305 Mulberry Street
St. Michaels, Maryland 21663
410-745-3737

St. Michaels Crab House and Marina had been the unloading site for millions of oysters and crabs distributed along the East Coast from Boston to the Carolinas. The building dates back to 1830 when it served as one of St. Michaels earliest oyster-shucking sheds. Specialties include steamed crabs, crab cakes, crab imperial, cream of crab bisque, and seafood chowder. Open daily for lunch and dinner. Credit cards: AE, DC, MC, and V.

Accommodations

■ BED AND BREAKFASTS

Barrett's B&B
204 N. Talbot Street
St. Michaels, Maryland 21663
410-745-3322

Parsonage Inn
210 Talbot Street
St. Michaels, Maryland 21663
410-745-5519

Hambleton Inn
202 Cherry Street
St. Michaels, Maryland 21663
410-745-3350

Two Swan Inn
Foot of Carpenter Street
St. Michaels, Maryland 21663
410-745-2929

Harris Cove Cottages
Route 579
Bozman, Maryland 21663
410-745-9701, 410-879-7672

Victoriana Inn
Foot of Cherry Street
P.O. Box 449
St. Michaels, Maryland 21663
410-745-3368

Kemp House
412 Talbot Street
P.O. Box 638
St. Michaels, Maryland 21663
410-745-2243

OSPREY

Also called a fish hawk, the osprey spends about half of the year around the Chesapeake Bay, arriving here on St. Patrick's Day from South America, where it winters.

Returning pairs of males and females usually find their old nest sites on trees or the red and green channel markers that guide boats through the rivers and harbors around the Bay. They repair their nests or build new ones of sticks. There they will incubate their eggs and care for their hatchlings until they are old enough to fly.

Osprey hover over the water looking for fish. They descend on their prey and grab it with their talons.

■ HOTELS, MOTELS, AND INNS

Harbourtowne
P.O. Box 126
Route 33
St. Michaels, Maryland 21663
410-745-9066, 800-446-9066

The Inn at Perry Cabin
308 Watkins Lane
P.O. Box 247
St. Michaels, Maryland 21663
410-745-5178

Pasadena Inn
P.O. Box 187
Route 329
Royal Oak, Maryland 21662
410-745-5053

St. Michaels Harbor Inn
101 North Harbor Road
St. Michaels, Maryland 21629
410-745-9001
800-955-9001

Wade's Point Inn
Route 33
P.O. Box 130
McDaniel, Maryland 21645
410-745-2500

TILGHMAN ISLAND

■ **BACKGROUND:** Settlers first visited the delicate shores of Tilghman Island in the 1600s. The current name honors Matthew Tilghman, known as the patriarch of Maryland. The island went through several names before arriving at Tilghman. These include Low's Island and Great Choptank Island. Today, Tilghman Island is a watermen's town with a fleet of skipjacks and one of the busiest draw bridges in the country.

Attractions

■ **VISITOR INFORMATION**

Talbot County Chamber of Commerce
805 Goldsborough Street
Easton, Maryland 21601
410-822-4606

■ **BOAT CHARTERS**

Harrison's Sport Fishing Center
U.S. Route 33
Tilghman, Maryland 21671
410-886-2123

Around 1900, Tilghman country was visited by people from across the United States coming by horse and buggy and steamboat to enjoy Captain Levin Harrison's hospitality and the excellent sports fishing. You are welcome to fish aboard one of their powerful Bay-built fishing boats. Their skilled captains will take you where the action is. "When I think of fishing, I always head for Harrison's." Fee.

■ BOAT CRUISES

Skipjack Cruises
Dogwood Harbor
Tilghman Island, Maryland
21663
410-745-6080

Come experience the Bay with Captain Ed Farley and let him share the lore of the "good old days". Set sail from Dogwood Harbor on this authentic working skipjack. Boarding the H.M. Krentz is stepping back into maritime history, catching a glimpse of the historic Eastern Shore when waterways were the means of travel and commerce and wind the source of power. Alternate schedules, full days and half-days, and points of departure are available upon request. Call for schedule and reservations. Fee.

■ SEASONAL EVENTS

Tilghman Island Day
Tilghman Island, Maryland
21671
410-886-2677

Exhibits of watermen's way of life, Bay seafood sold at the firehouse, tours of the famous skipjack fleet, workboat races, and auctions. Held mid-October, 10 a.m. to 6 p.m. Admission charge.

Tilghman Island Seafood Festival
Main Street
Tilghman Island, Maryland
21671
410-886-2677

Festival includes all kinds of seafood prepared the Tilghman Island way. Games, rides, and parades are offered. Held in late June. Free.

Restaurants

One way that Baytrippers can really get a taste for the Eastern Shore is to walk the islands' docks, talk to the watermen, and use cameras to investigate the Bay's traditional way of life.

Bay Hundred Restaurant
Route 33 and Knapps Narrow
Tilghman, Maryland 21671
410-886-2622

House specialties at Bay Hundred—the old name given to the southern end of the Eastern Shore region—include the seafood combination platter, fresh fish of the day, shrimp scampi, incredible crab cakes, delicious soft shell crabs, stir fried shrimp, crab soup Maryland style, crab salad, roasted oysters, and oyster stew. Open for lunch and dinner daily. Credit cards: MC and V.

Chesapeake Landing
Route 33
McDaniel, Maryland 21647
410-745-9600

Located mid-way between St. Michaels and Tilghman Island, Chesapeake Landing is a great place to stop if you yearn for the specialties of the Eastern Shore. The crabmeat, oysters, hard crabs, and soft crabs come directly from the water to you. Many of the dishes are local favorites whose recipes have been passed down through the years. Open daily for lunch and dinner. Credit cards: MC and V.

CHESAPEAKE BAY STEAMED CRABS
Served Hot & Spicy All Year Round
Priced Daily

Harrison's Chesapeake House
Route 33
Tilghman Island, Maryland
21671
410-886-2123

Harrison's, as well as being a sports fishing center with a fleet of 14 charter fishing boats, also has lodging facilities. The oldest part of the inn was built in 1876. My favorite spot is one of the three waterfront dining rooms offering southern cuisine created by the Harrison family for over three generations. Enjoy meals such as fried chicken and crab cakes with fresh vegetables and homemade bread. Or try the great soft shell crab sandwich or the oyster buffet which includes oysters served eight ways. Open daily for breakfast, lunch, and dinner. Credit cards: MC and V.

The Tilghman Inn
Coopertown Road
Tilghman Island,Maryland
21671
410-885-2141

During the War of 1812, the British captured and held Tilghman Island as a supply base. Long before that, the Choptank Indians claimed the island. Today the island's seafood is the county's most important product. Be part of that tradition and seek out the Tilghman Inn. House specialties include crab meat cocktail, sherried crab bisque, stuffed oysters mornay, crab cakes, stuffed soft shell crabs, and wonderful crab imperial. Open daily for lunch and dinner. Credit cards: AE, MC, and V.

OYSTERS
RAW
&
STEAMED

Accommodations

■ BED AND BREAKFASTS

Black Walnut Point Inn
P.O. Box 308
Black Walnut Road
Tilghman Island, Maryland 21671
410-886-2452

Grandview Cottages
Ball Creek
Neavitt, Maryland 21652
410-745-5069

The Lazy Jack Inn
5907 Tilghman Island Road
Tilghman Island, Maryland 21671
410-886-2215

Sinclair House
5718 Black Walnut Point Road
Tilghman Island, Maryland 21671
410-886-2147

Wood Duck Inn
Gibsontown Road
Tilghman Island, Maryland 21671
410-886-2070

DOGWOOD HARBOR EXHIBITS

- WATERMEN GAMES
- BOAT DOCKING CONTEST
- SKIPJACKS
- HAND TONGING
- OYSTER DIVING
- CLAM BOATS
- PATENT TONG BOAT
- MARYLAND WATERMENS ASSN. EXHIBIT

TILGHMAN ISLAND DAY

■ HOTELS, MOTELS, AND INNS

Harrison's Country Inn
Route 33
Tilghman Island, Maryland
21671
410-886-2123

Tilghman Island Inn
Coopertown Road
Tilghman Island, Maryland
21671
410-886-2141

OXFORD

■ **BACKGROUND:** Oxford, one of the oldest towns in Maryland, marks the year 1683 as its official beginning. In that year, Oxford was named by the Maryland general assembly as a seaport and laid out as a town. Until the American Revolution, Oxford enjoyed prominence as an international shipping center surrounded by wealthy tobacco plantations. The American Revolution marked the end of Oxford's glory, and it wasn't until after the Civil War that the town reemerged as a shipper of seafood to markets all across the country.

Attractions

■ **VISITOR INFORMATION**

Talbot County Chamber of Commerce
805 Goldsborough Street
Easton, Maryland 21601
410-822-4606

■ **BOAT CRUISES**

Bellevue Ferry
North Morris Street and the Strand
Oxford, Maryland 21654
410-745-9023

This ferry, believed to be the oldest privately operated ferry in the country, began service in 1683. It temporarily halted service after the American Revolution, resumed in 1836, and has been in continuous use since that time. Open May to Labor Day, Monday through Friday, 7 a.m. to 9 p.m.; and Saturday and Sunday, 9 a.m. to 9 p.m. From Labor Day to April, open Monday through Friday, 7 a.m. to sunset, and Saturday and Sunday, 9 a.m. to sunset. Closed Christmas through February. Toll.

Oxford Customs House
Morris Street and the Strand
Oxford, Maryland 21654
410-226-5122

The Oxford Customs House is an exact replica of the first Federal Customs House in the United States. The original was built when George Washington appointed Jeremiah Banning as the first customs agent in 1791 after the Revolutionary War. The model was created as a bicentennial project in 1976. Open mid-April to mid-October; Friday, Saturday, and Sunday, 2 p.m. to 5 p.m.; and by appointment. Free.

■ **MUSEUMS**

Oxford Museum
Morris and Market Streets
Oxford, Maryland 21654
410-226-5122

Nineteenth century maritime history exhibits with emphasis on Oxford's early history. Open Friday, Saturday, Sunday, 2 p.m. to 5 p.m.; and by appointment. Donations appreciated.

Restaurants

Pope's Tavern
Morris Street (at the head
of the town dock)
Oxford, Maryland 21654
410-226-5220

You will enjoy creative cuisine
and a cosy atmosphere at Pope's
Tavern, nationally acclaimed in
gourmet and country inn magazines. Open for lunch and dinner. Closed Tuesdays. Credit
cards: MC and V.

The Masthead
Miller Street
Oxford, Maryland 21654
410-226-5303

The Masthead offers a small
jewel of a dining room adjoin-
ing the friendly local pub. Featured are fresh fish innovatively
prepared, surprise sauces, and
crisp local vegetables, accompa-
nied by fine wines. Open for
lunch and dinner. Credit cards:
MC and V.

The Robert Morris Inn
Morris Street and the Strand
Oxford, Maryland 21654
410-226-5111

Quality seafood is served in the
colonial charm of a historic inn
on the Tred Avon River. James
A. Michener, author of *Chesapeake*, rated this inn's crab cakes
as the best of any restaurant on
the Eastern Shore. Open for
breakfast, lunch, and dinner.
Credit cards: MC and V.

"Stand at the corner of the Robert Morris Inn and look out over
the water. In the 17th and 18th
centuries one could see large ships
from England and other parts of
the Colonies at anchor. They
brought things necessary for the
Oxford residents and took tobacco
back to England."

Accommodations

■ **BED AND BREAKFASTS**

The 1876 House
110 North Morris Street
Oxford, Maryland 21654
410-226-5496

Oxford Inn
Morris Street
Oxford, Maryland 21654
410-226-5220

■ **HOTELS, MOTELS, AND INNS**

The Robert Morris Inn
Morris Street and the Strand
Oxford, Maryland 21654
410-226-4111

MIDDLE BAY

Cambridge to Pocomoke City

Follow the water....

- Cambridge
- Salisbury
- Princess Anne
- Crisfield
- Snow Hill
- Pocomoke City

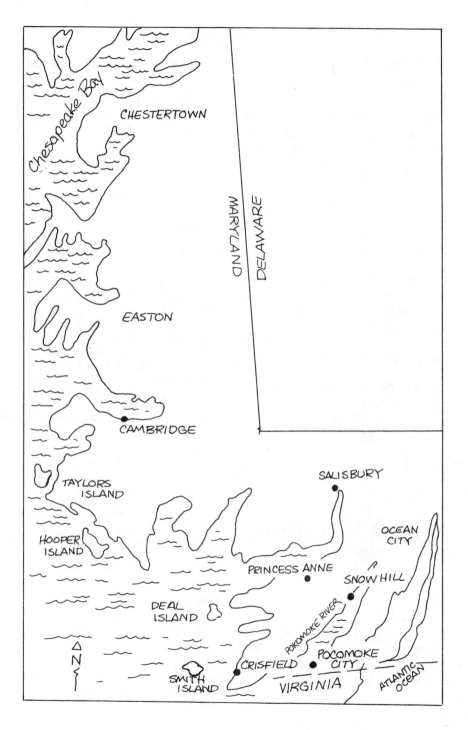

CAMBRIDGE

■ **BACKGROUND:** Cambridge was founded in 1684 by an act of the General Assembly. Many of its earliest citizens were aristocratic Englishmen. It is believed that Cambridge University in England inspired its name. In the 18th century Cambridge was a trading center where tobacco, seafood, and muskrat pelts could be bought. Even after tobacco declined, Cambridge grew steadily. Today it's the second largest city on the Maryland coastline.

Attractions

■ **VISITOR INFORMATION**

Dorchester County Tourism
501 Court Lane
Cambridge, Maryland 21613
410-228-1000

■ **AIRPORT**

Cambridge/Dorchester Airport
5223 Bucktown Road
Cambridge, Maryland 21613
410-228-4571

■ **BOAT CRUISES**

Nathan of Dorchester
526 Poplar Street
Cambridge, Maryland 21613
410-228-1000

Baytrippers should look for the opening the **SAILWINDS PARK VISITORS CENTER.** When completed in 1996, the 14,500-square-foot center will include tourist information services, a 125-seat theater, and displays that will highlight Maryland history. An observation deck will overlook a restored wetlands area and offer panoramic views of the Choptank River.

Nathan of Dorchester is a 45' wooden boat modeled after the working skipjack used at the turn of the century. The boat is being used to showcase Dorchester's maritime heritage and to educate the public on traditional means of wooden shipbuilding and seafood dredging, a way of life in historical Dorchester County. Call for cruise information. Fee.

■ FISHING

Choptank Fishing Pier
Route 50
Cambridge, Maryland 21613

Increased traffic along Route 50 resulted in a new bridge. Thanks to the Maryland Department of Natural Resources, the old bridge was retained and transformed in to a fishing pier. With no vehicles allowed on the bridge, it has become Maryland's longest fishing pier—6,000 feet end-to-end—and the first to be designed and run by the state specifically for fishing. Free.

■ HISTORIC TOWNS

Hooper Island
Route 335
Hooper Island, Maryland 21634

Hooper Island is actually comprised of three islands: the upper, middle, and lower islands. Some properties were part of the earliest land grants in Dorchester County. Settlers came from St. Mary's County, across the Bay. One of the first, Henry Hooper, owned much of the land, and the islands were probably named after him. The upper island has two small villages. Honga, named for the river which bounds the island on the east. The second village is Fishing Creek. The middle island, accessed by the spectacular Narrows Ferry Bridge, is sparsely settled except within the village of Hoopersville. The lower island is no longer inhabited and can only be reached by boat.

Historic Towns, cont.

Taylors Island
Route 16
Taylors Island, Maryland 21669

Named by John Taylor in 1662, the town consists of several islands separated by Slaughter Creek, which twists southward to the Honga River. History flourishes here, with local pirates, Dutch shipwrecks, Spanish coins, and battles with the British. At the lower end of Slaughter Creek lies a small wildlife management area.

Town of East New Market
Route 14
East New Market, Maryland 21631
410-228-3234
410-228-3575

Settled in 1660, the town is graced by many fine homes including Friendship Hall, Maurice Manor, Smith Cottage, House of the Hinges, and the New Market House. Self-guided tour available. Free.

Town of Secretary
Route 16
Secretary, Maryland 21664

Secretary began during the time of the proprietary governorships of Maryland in 1661. While in Maryland, Lord Dewall served as Secretary to the Province of Maryland. In his honor, his land was named "Secretary."

Town of Vienna
Route 50
Vienna, Maryland 21869
410-228-3575
410-228-3234

Site of an Indian settlement called Emperor's Landing in the 17th century. Historic homes located along Water Street include the home of Governor Thomas Holiday Hicks. He thwarted efforts of legislators who would have denounced the union and seceded to the Confederacy. Free self-guided walking tours available.

■ HUNTING

Herb Hastings
Route 1, Box 2
Cambridge, Maryland 21613
410-228-7252

Waterfowling in Maryland is an Eastern Shore tradition. This region is the winter capital of the Canada goose. Maryland has the greatest concentration of geese of any state on the Atlantic flyway. Both field and water hunting are available. Goose hunting mid-November to the end of January; duck hunting mid-November to mid-January. No Sunday hunting in Maryland. Fee.

91

■ MISCELLANEOUS

Brewery Tour
Wild Goose Brewery
20 Washington Street
Cambridge, Maryland 21613
410-221-1121

The Wild Goose Brewery was established in the summer of 1989 and is located on the site of the old Phillips Packing Company plant, where they once canned everything from oysters to C-rations. The brewing plant has a production capacity of 150 barrels a week. Groups are welcome. Guided tours last about one hour and include a little taste. Individuals can tour free. Admission charge for groups. Open Monday through Friday.

Spocott Windmill
Route 343
Cambridge, Maryland 21613
410-228-7090

Authentic reproduction of a post windmill, the type early, 17th-century American colonists used in the Chesapeake Bay region. A small miller's house and an 1868 one-room schoolhouse were moved here and restored. Open daily, 10 a.m. to 5 p.m. Free.

Blackwater National Wildlife Refuge
3216 Key Wallace Drive
Cambridge, Maryland 21613
410-228-2677

Blackwater Wildlife Refuge harbors 250 bird species and is a chief wintering area for Canada geese and ducks. It is also a haven for three of the nation's endangered species—the bald eagle, Delmarva fox squirrel, and the peregrine falcon. Baytrippers can take a self-guided car tour along a five-mile wildlife drive that loops around the marsh. The refuge is open daily, 7:30 a.m. to 4 p.m. Closed major holidays. Free.

■ MUSEUMS

Brannock Maritime Museum
210 Talbot Avenue
P.O. Box 337
Cambridge, Maryland 21613
410-228-6838

This exhibit centering on whaling ships reminds visitors of the area's importance in shipbuilding during the fascinating era of sail. Also of interest is a display on the first steamboats. An entire room is dedicated to the steamboats that called on the port of Cambridge. Open Saturday and Sunday, 1 p.m. to 4 p.m. Also by appointment. Free.

Dorchester Heritage Museum
Route 343
Cambridge, Maryland 21613
410-228-4924
410-228-6172

Features a display on Dorchester County's history. Early aircraft, farming, nature, and Indian exhibits. Open Saturday and Sunday, 1 p.m. to 4:30 p.m. Also by appointment. Free.

Museums, cont.

Meredith House and Neild Museum
902 LaGrange Avenue
Cambridge, Maryland 21613
410-228-7953

Exhibits of seven Maryland governors, a farm museum, and a smoke house from the early 1700's. The Meredith House is a late 18th century plantation home. Upstairs, you will enjoy the old dolls and baby buggy collection. Also of note is the smokehouse, reputed to be the oldest building in the county. Open Thursday through Saturday, 10 a.m. to 4 p.m.; Sundays, 1:30 p.m. to 4:30 p.m. Also by appointment. Admission charge.

Taylors Island Museum
Route 16
Taylors Island, Maryland 21669
410-397-3338
410-397-3262

The old school, circa 1916, has been converted to a museum to showcase local and regional antiques and memorabilia. Open by appointment. Free.

■ PARKS AND GARDENS

Dorchester County Historical Society
902 LaGrange Avenue
Cambridge, Maryland 21613
410-228-7953

Colonial-style garden demonstrates the many uses of herbs—for cooking, beauty, and health.

■ SEASONAL EVENTS

National Outdoor Show
K-8 School
Golden Hill
Cambridge, Maryland 21613
410-397-3517

This festival features a muskrat-skinning contest, log sawing, arts and crafts, wildlife artists, and plenty of oysters and crabs. Held late February. Admission charge.

Seafood Feast-i-val
Horn Point Road
Cambridge, Maryland 21613
410-228-3575

The Chamber of Commerce's annual seafood festival offers an exciting menu of steamed crabs, homemade crab cakes, homemade crab soup, fried clam strips, fresh fried fish, corn-on-the cob, sliced tomatoes, ranch fries, chilled watermelon, cold soft drinks, and beer. It's all held on the shores of the Choptank River at the University of Maryland's Horn Point Marine Research Lab. Held mid-August. Admission charge.

Strawberry Festival
Route 343
Cambridge, Maryland 21613
410-228-7807

This festival features strawberries by the quart, strawberry cakes and ice cream, BBQ'd chicken, homemade soups, a sweet shop, and a flea market. Held early June. Free.

Warwick River Fest
Secretary Boat Ramp
Secretary, Maryland 21664
410-943-3842

"The biggest party in Dorchester County." Festivities include a parade, raft race, entertainment, carnival games, and food concessions. Held early September. Free.

Restaurants

Gale Winds
203 Trenton Street
Cambridge, Maryland 21613
410-221-1086

You will enjoy the gentle breezes at the Gale Wind Restaurant and Marina located on Cambridge Creek. My visit recalls Maryland style crab soup. It arrived hot and spicy, just the way I like it. The fresh, soft crab sandwich was so good I could have eaten two more. Open daily for lunch and dinner.

Suicide Bridge Restaurant
Suicide Bridge Road
Secretary, Maryland 21643
410-943-4689

House specialties include fresh rock fish, creamy crab dip, summer squash casserole, stuffed potatoes with cheese, and steamed crabs—all this and a lovely view, too. Open for lunch and dinner. Closed Monday. Credit cards: MC and V.

Accommodations

■ BED AND BREAKFASTS

Commodore's Cottage
210 Talbot Avenue
Cambridge, Maryland 21613
410-228-6938

Glasgow on the Choptank
1500 Hambrooks Boulevard
Cambridge, Maryland 21613
410-228-0575

Edmondson House
Main Street
East New Market, Maryland 21631
410-943-4471

Governor's Ordinary
Water Street
Vienna, Maryland 21869
410-376-3530

Lodgecliffe on the Choptank
103 Choptank Terrace
Cambridge, Maryland 21613
410-228-1760

Nanticoke Manor House
Church and Water Streets
P.O. Box 248
Vienna, Maryland 21869
410-376-3530

Oakley House
906 Locust Street
Cambridge, Maryland 21613
410-228-6623

Sarke Plantation
6033 Todd Point Road
Cambridge, Maryland 21613
410-228-7020

The Tavern House
111 Water Street
Vienna, Maryland 21869
410-376-3347

■ CAMPING

Madison Bay Campground
P.O. Box 33, Route 16
Madison, Maryland 21648
410-228-4111

Taylors Island Campgrounds
P.O. Box 156
Taylors Island, Maryland 21669
410-397-3275

Tideland Park Campground
Route 16
Taylors Island, Maryland 21669
410-397-3473

■ HOTELS, MOTELS, AND INNS

Bay Country Motel
Route 50
East Cambridge, Maryland 21613
410-225-4444

Econo Lodge
Route 50
East Cambridge, Maryland 21613
410-221-0800

Quality Inn
Route 50 East
Cambridge, Maryland 21613
410-228-6900

Talbot Landing Motel
Route 50
East Trappe, Maryland 21673
410-476-3189

SALISBURY

■ **BACKGROUND:** Salisbury was laid out as a town in 1732. It's believed that the community was named after a city in England. Today, the town is the hub of the poultry, farming, and finance industries of the Delmarva peninsula.

Attractions

■ **VISITOR INFORMATION**

Wicomico County Convention and Visitor's Bureau
500 Glen Avenue Extended
Salisbury, Maryland 21801
410-548-4914
800-332-TOUR

■ **AIRPORT**

Salisbury-Wicomico Airport
Route 4, Airport Road
Salisbury, Maryland 21801
410-548-4827

■ **BOAT CRUISES**

Maryland Lady
P.O. Box 316
313 West Main Street
Salisbury, Maryland 21801
410-543-2466

Enjoy a cruise on the Wicomico River. The Maryland Lady will transport you back in time to those days when paddle wheelers cruised the Wicomico River. It's an exciting experience for the entire family. Call for your cruise information. Open Monday through Saturday. Admission charge.

Upper Ferry
Upper Ferry Road
Salisbury, Maryland 21840
410-548-4873

Outboard diesel-powered ferry guided by cable across the Wicomico River. Carries two cars and foot passengers. Open daily. Free.

Whitehaven Ferry
Route 352
Whitehaven, Maryland 21840
410-548-4873

This ferry has operated here continuously since 1690. The cable ferry crosses the Wicomico River between Wicomico and Somerset Counties; it carries three cars and foot passengers. Open daily; seasonal hours. Free.

■ MISCELLANEOUS

Salisbury Pewter
Route 13
North Salisbury, Maryland 21801
410-546-1188

Formed in 1980 by a small group of investors who wanted to see the art of making pewter by hand kept alive. Show room, gift shop. Guided tour by a pointment. Monday through Friday, 9 a.m. to 4:30 p.m. Saturday, 9 a.m. to 4 p.m. Free.

Salisbury Zoological Park
City Park
750 South Park Drive
Salisbury, Maryland 21801
410-548-3188

This compact, 12-acre zoo is nestled on the banks of a branch of the Wicomico River. Shade trees, exotic plantings, and the wildlife offer a cool, peaceful setting for family outings. Open Memorial Day through Labor Day, 8 a.m. to 7:30 p.m.; the rest of the year, 8 a.m. to 4:30 p.m. Free.

■ MUSEUMS

Nutter's Museum
North Division Street
Fruitland, Maryland 21826
410-749-2677

This is the last building in the county used solely as voting house. It's been converted to a museum for local, state, and national political Americana. Changing exhibits. Open May through September, Thursdays, 10 a.m. to 4 p.m. Free.

Pemberton Hall
Pemberton Drive
Salisbury, Maryland 21801
410-742-3408
410-749-2677

Built in 1741, Pemberton Hall was the home of Colonel Isaac Handy, prominent local citizen of the revolutionary period and founder of Salisbury. Listed on the National Register of Historical Places. Open Sundays, 2 p.m. to 4 p.m.; May through October or by appointment. Admission charge.

Poplar Hill Mansion
117 Elizabeth Street
Salisbury, Maryland 21801
410-749-1776

Federal-style house built by Major Levin Handy. Features pilasters in the main entrance and palladian windows. Cornice of the living room outstanding. Open Sunday, 1 p.m. to 4 p.m. or by appointment. Free.

Ward Museum of Wildfowl Art
909 Schumaker Drive
Salisbury, Maryland 21801
410-742-4988

See wood come alive in this unique display of wildfowl carvings, representing the top works of the finest contemporary carvers and the best classic hunting decoys in the nation. Open Tuesday through Saturday, 10 a.m. to 5 p.m. Open Sunday, 1 p.m. to 5 p.m. Admission charge.

■ PARKS AND GARDENS

Pemberton Park
Pemberton Drive
Salisbury, Maryland 21801
410-742-3115

Take the time to walk the Wicomico River. The park offers nature trails with interpretive signs, a picnic area, pond, and educational programs. Open daily from dawn to dusk. Free.

River Walk Park
Salisbury, Maryland 21801
410-749-0144

Charming, meandering walk along Salisbury's downtown Wicomico River front. Free.

■ SEASONAL EVENTS

Chesapeake Migration Festival
500 Glen Avenue
Salisbury, Maryland 21801
410-548-4914

Annual fall art exhibit and sale. Features of this fall celebration include an antique decoy auction and wildfowl art. Early October. Admission charge.

Pemberton Colonial Fair
Pemberton Drive
Salisbury, Maryland 21801
410-742-3115

A unique event based on 18th century life held at Pemberton Historical Park in Salisbury. Music, games, and sports; arts and crafts; antiques; horse and carriage parade; and hunt club exhibit. Also includes classes and demonstrations of 18th century crafts, a magician, dancers, and period food. Early October. Free.

Salisbury Festival
P.O. Box 510
Downtown Plaza
Salisbury, Maryland 21803
410-749-0144

Three-day celebration in downtown Salisbury. Arts and crafts exhibits, entertainment, raft race, block party, antique sports cars, food, bicycle race, 10K run, and children's activities. Early May. Free.

Restaurants

Captain's Galley
803 So. Salisbury Blvd.
Salisbury, Maryland 21801
410-860-1636

The crab cakes that brought world acclaim to Crisfield, Maryland, are now available in Salisbury. The Captain's Galley is located next to the Giant Food Store. It doesn't offer the view of Tangier Sound, but the taste is here. Open for breakfast, lunch and dinner.

English's Restaurant
735 South Salisbury
Boulevard
Salisbury, Maryland 21801
410-742-8183

English's is a chain of family-style restaurants featuring Eastern Shore cooking such as crabs, steak, and chicken. Open for breakfast, lunch, and dinner.

Red Roost
Clara Road
Whitehaven, Maryland 21873
410-546-5443

The Red Roost cooks up blue crabs steamed scarlet in spicy Chesapeake brine for informal feasts. Add hush puppies, corn on the cob, and fried chicken, and you have created the best in Chesapeake Bay cuisine. Open daily for dinner.

Watermen's Cove Restaurant
925 Snow Hill Road
Salisbury, Maryland 21801
410-546-1400

Try Watermen's Cove's deluxe steamed combo, featuring shrimp, clams, scallops, fish, and oysters. It's nature's best. Open daily for lunch and dinner. Credit cards: MC and V.

Accommodations

■ BED AND BREAKFASTS

White Oak Inn
804 Spring Hill Road
Salisbury, Maryland 21801
410-742-4887

■ CAMPING

Roaring Point
Waterfront Campground
P.O. Box B
Nanticoke, Maryland 21840
410-873-2553

Sandy Hill Family Camp
Route 1 P.O. Box 93
Quantico, Maryland 21875
410-896-2979

■ HOTELS, MOTELS, AND INNS

Comfort Inn Salisbury
U.S. 13 North
Salisbury, Maryland 21801
410-543-4666

Howard Johnson Lodge
U.S. 13 North and Route 6
Salisbury, Maryland 21801
410-742-5195

Days Inn Salisbury
U.S. 13 North
Salisbury, Maryland 21801
410-749-6200

Sheraton Inn Salisbury
300 South Salisbury Boulevard
Salisbury, Maryland 21801
410-546-4400

Hampton Inn
1735 North Salisbury Boulevard
Salisbury, Maryland 21801
410-546-1300

Super 8 Motel
2615 North Salisbury Boulevard
Salisbury, Maryland 21801
410-749-5131

Holiday Inn Salisbury
U.S. 13 North and
Salisbury Bypass
Salisbury, Maryland 21801
410-742-7194

Thrift Travel Inn
603 North Salisbury Boulevard
Salisbury, Maryland 21801
410-742-5135

PRINCESS ANNE

■ **BACKGROUND:** Princess Anne dates back to 1732 when the Maryland Assembly agreed to purchase 24 acres along the Manokin River. This new port-of-entry was called Princess Anne as a tribute to the daughter of King George II. In 1744, the town became Somerset's county seat and remains so today. Princess Anne is charming and her brick walkways and meandering sidewalks invite Baytrippers to stroll, coaxing admirers to appreciate her many beauty spots.

Attractions

■ **VISITOR INFORMATION**

Princess Anne Chamber of Commerce
Box 642
Princess Anne, Maryland 21853
410-651-2961

Somerset County Tourism
P.O. Box 243, Route 13
Princess Anne, Maryland 21853
410-651-2968
800-521-9189

■ **HISTORIC SITES**

Fairmount Academy
Route 361
Upper Fairmount, Maryland 21867
410-651-0351
410-651-3291

Founded in 1839, the two-story, gothic revival style Fairmount Academy was a private school until 1969. Today, it is the last 19th century schoolhouse standing in Somerset County. Open by appointment. Free.

**Princess Anne
Historic District**
Route 675
Princess Anne, Maryland 21853
410-521-9189

Princess Anne is surpassed only by Annapolis in the number of its national historic registered homes built in the early 18th and 19th centuries. The historic district includes Manokin Presbyterian Church (1765), Tunstall Cottage (about 1733), and St. Andrew's Episcopal Church (1770). Free self-guided walking tour brochure available.

Teackle Mansion
Prince William Street
Princess Anne, Maryland 21853
410-651-1705
410-651-2968

This building is an imposing pink brick copy of a Scottish manor house. Its drawing room features an elaborate plaster ceiling; its kitchen boasts a 7-foot fireplace with beehive oven. Open Sundays, 2 to 4 p.m. Admission charge.

■ HISTORIC TOWNS

Deal Island
Route 363
Deal Island, Maryland 21821

Would you like to watch local watermen unload their day's catch, observe a soft shell crab shedding operation, see how an oyster hatchery works, watch crab pickers' fingers fly, take pictures of a skipjack, and sample a soft shell crab sandwich or homemade crab cake at the local deli? You can do it all at Deal Island Harbor. Park the car and enjoy. Take a drive on the island; it's only three miles long.

■ **SEASONAL EVENTS**

Labor Day Skipjack Races
Route 363
Deal Island, Maryland 21821
410-784-2428

This festival is held on Labor Day weekend and includes a crab feast, canoe race, fishing tournament, crab pot pull contest, swimming contest, small and large boat docking contest, helicopter rides, food, drink, and plenty of recreation. Above all, everyone comes to see the famous skipjack races. Labor Day. Admission charge.

Olde Princess Anne Days
P.O. Box 242
Princess Anne, Maryland 21853
410-651-1705

Many of the town's historical homes are open to the public during the town festival held in the middle of October. Admission charge.

Restaurants

Island Seafood Deli
Route 363
Deal Island, Maryland 21821
410-784-2543

While on Deal Island, be sure to stop at this popular seafood deli. Along with subs, pizza, ice cream, and salads, there is my favorite—freshly prepared soft shell crabs and delicious crab cakes.   Open for lunch and dinner.

Peaky's Restaurant
Route 13 and
Mt. Vernon Road
Princess Anne, Maryland 21853
410-651-1950

Peaky's has added many new and delicious items to their already delectable menu. The fare includes homemade pasta, fresh veal dishes, delicious seafood specialties, and exciting desserts, just to name a few. Open for lunch and dinner. Credits cards: MC and V.

Accommodations

■ BED AND BREAKFASTS

Elmwood
Locust Point Road
Princess Anne, Maryland 21853
410-651-1066

Hyland House
Route 3 P.O. Box 144
Princess Anne, Maryland 21853
410-651-1056

Hayman House
117 Prince William Street
Princess Anne, Maryland 21853
410-651-2753

■ CAMPING

Lake Somerset Campground
U.S. Route 13
Westover, Maryland 21871
410-957-1866
410-957-9897

Princess Anne Campground
U.S. Route 13
Princess Anne, Maryland 21853
410-651-1520

■ HOTELS, MOTELS, AND INNS

Econo Lodge, Princess Anne
Route 13
Princess Anne, Maryland 21853
410-651-9400

Princess Anne Motel
Route 3
Princess Anne, Maryland 21853
410-651-1900

Washington Hotel Inn
Somerset Avenue
Princess Anne, Maryland 21853
410-651-2525

ISLAND SEAFOOD
DELI
SUBS
PIZZA
SOFT CRABS
CRAB CAKES
SALADS
ICE CREAM
DAILY SPECIALS

CRISFIELD

■ **BACKGROUND:** Back in 1667, the original English settlers of the area adopted the Indian name, Annemessex, meaning "bountiful waters" for their community. The first little settlement prospered in relative isolation for 200 years, evolving into a fishing village known as Somers Cove. When the railroad was extended to the harbor in 1867, thanks to the efforts of John Crisfield, the inhabitants began to enjoy regular mail delivery. It was the railroad, providing immediate transportation for the Bay's incredible oyster harvest, that built Crisfield into a boisterous boomtown reminiscent of gold rush communities of the old west. Although crabbing has replaced oystering as the foundation for the local seafood industry, Crisfield still proudly calls itself "The Crab Capital of the World."

Attractions

■ **VISITOR INFORMATION**

Crisfield Chamber of Commerce
P.O. Box 291
Crisfield, Maryland 21817
410-968-2500
800-782-3913

Somerset County Tourism Commission
P.O. Box 243
Princess Anne, Maryland 21853
410-651-2968
800-521-9189

■ **AIRPORT**

Crisfield Airport
4784 Jacksonville Road
Crisfield, Maryland 21817
410-968-1572

■ BOAT CRUISES

Capt. Alan Tyler
Somers Cove Marina
Crisfield, Maryland 21817
410-425-2771

Smith Island is Maryland's only inhabited island accessible exclusively by boat. Comprised of three separate villages named Ewell, Tylerton, and Rhodes Point, Smith Island lies in the Chesapeake Bay 12 miles west of Crisfield. History records that Captain John Smith visited in the year 1608, came ashore here, and gave the island his name. Seven days a week in season, the ferry leaves from Somers Cove Marina, Crisfield, at 12:30 p.m. and arrives back at Crisfield at 5:15 p.m. Fee.

Capt. Rudy Thomas
10th and Main Streets
Crisfield, Maryland 21817
410-968-2338
800-863-2338

Your cruise features a narrated tour along the world's oldest and largest naval base. You'll see naval vessels of every description from giant aircraft carriers to sleek submarines. This exciting Chesapeake Bay package includes a 4-hour cruise from Crisfield to Portsmouth on Saturday, with buffet lunch; one night at the Holiday Inn in Portsmouth; breakfast on Sunday; and a return cruise back to Crisfield on Sunday afternoon. Reservations required. Fee.

Boat Cruises, cont.

Island Princess
10th and Main Streets
Ewell, Maryland 21824
410-968-3206

Cruise with Capt. Otis Ray Tyler aboard the Island Princess. Your Smith Island cruise departs from the city dock at the foot of Main Street, Crisfield. The boat leaves Crisfield at 12:30 p.m. and arrives at Smith Island at 1:15 p.m. Returning, it sets out from Smith Island at 4:00 p.m. and arrives at Crisfield at 5:00 p.m. Daily cruises, including Sunday. Fee.

Tangier Island Cruises
10th and Main Streets
Crisfield, Maryland 21817
410-968-2338
800-863-2338

Visit charming and historic Tangier Island, Virginia, on the most modern cruise ship in the Chesapeake Bay, the "Steven Thomas". Tangier Island lies 14 miles west of Crisfield, Maryland. Little has changed since its first European settlement. Once on the island you'll find no traffic, noise or blaring car stereos. The "Steven Thomas" departs daily (including Sundays), May 15th through October, from the city dock on Main Street in Crisfield. Your cruise leaves Crisfield at 12:30 p.m. and arrives at Tangier at 1:45 p.m. Your return cruise leaves Tangier at 4:00 p.m. and arrives at Crisfield at 5:15 p.m. Fee.

■ BOAT CHARTERS

Charter Fishing Center
P.O. Box 67, 7th Street
Crisfield, Maryland 21817
410-968-0925
800-967-3474

Somers Cove Marina is the perfect marina for boating, sailing, and fishing on the Chesapeake Bay, Tangier, and Pocomoke Sounds. Charter boats, head-boats, and new stainless steel fish-cleaning stations. Call for information and free fishing map. Fee.

"The Caroline D" II
10711 Riverton Road
Mardela Springs, Maryland
21837
410-742-7762

Charter boat captains can be counted on to locate the "big ones" and a knowledgeable captain is worth his weight in bait and tackle. I like Capt. Gerald Dawson and his simple approach to fishing the bay. "Whatever's biting good is what we like to catch." Seasonal. Call for your schedule. Fee.

■ MISCELLANEOUS

Carvel Hall
Route 413
Crisfield, Maryland 21817
410-968-0500

You'll enjoy your visit to this factory outlet company featuring heirloom-quality, Carvel Hall cutlery and seafood tools manufactured right here in their Crisfield factory. Open daily from 10 a.m. to 6 p.m. Closed major holidays. Free.

Sky Tours
4784 Jacksonville Road
Crisfield, Maryland 21817
410-968-1572

Touch the clouds, skim the seas, set your imagination free. View Smith Island, Tangier Island, and the Blackwater Refuge from high above the water. Open daily. Fee.

■ MUSEUMS

Early American Museum
Hudson's Corner
Marion Station, Maryland 21817
410-623-8324<

The Burgess Country Store is truly a replica of the past. Bathed in a 19th century atmosphere, it is an authentic general store which was the social center of many small towns during the past century. Its shelves and counters hold many long-forgotten items, some still in their original packaging. Open Thursday through Sunday, 10 a.m. to 5 p.m., year round. Admission charge.

Tawes Historic Museum
Main Street
Crisfield, Maryland 21817
410-968-2501

Exhibits pertaining to the late governor, J. Millard Tawes (1958 to 1966), history and development of the Crisfield seafood industry, local art and folklore, and life of the area from Indian times to present. Open daily, March 1 through November, 10 a.m. to 4 p.m. Admission charge.

■ PARKS AND GARDENS

Janes Island State Park
6280 Alfred Lawson Drive
Crisfield, Maryland 21817
410-974-3683

Janes Island State Park has been designed with the nature lover in mind. Complete facilities for any type of camping. Cabin rentals. Boating facilities available. A nicer park cannot be found. Admission charge.

■ SEASONAL EVENTS

Hard Crab Derby
Somers Cove Marina
Crisfield, Maryland 21817
410-968-2500

AND THE WINNER IS.....
CRISFIELD BILL

The Hard Crab Derby has been held annually for over 40 years with three days of festivities to entertain the entire family. The weekend consists of crab-racing, boat-docking, boat-racing, parade, cooking contest, crab-picking contest, a beauty pageant, and arts and crafts. All of this is featured along with many types of delightful food. Held Labor Day weekend. Admission charge.

J. Millard Tawes Crab and Clam Bake
Somers Cove Marina
Crisfield, Maryland 21817
410-968-2500

This annual crab and clam bake is held the 3rd Wednesday of July. The menu consists of all-you-can-eat crabs, clams, and a variety of other Eastern Shore delicacies. Reservations required. Admission charge.

Watermen's Folklife Festival
Somers Cove Marina
Crisfield, Maryland 21817
410-968-2500

All kinds of crafts are demonstrated here and many local artists' works are on display. Also enjoy clowns, food, horse-and-buggy rides, a silent auction. Held late July 10 a.m. to 6 p.m. Free.

Restaurants

Bayside Inn
Rhodes Point
Smith Island, Maryland 21824
410-425-2771

The Bayside Inn overlooks Rhodes Point Harbor. Hardy, family-style meals include crab cakes, clam fritters, ham, corn pudding, homemade apple sauce, custard pies, and plenty more. Open for lunch and dinner.

Captain's Galley
Main Street
Crisfield, Maryland 21817
410-968-1636

Captain's Galley restaurant is one of Crisfield's best known restaurants and, without a doubt, home of the "world's best crab cake," as defined by several national magazines. They offer a wide variety of regional seafood dishes, soups, and sandwiches. Children's menu available. Open daily for breakfast, lunch, and dinner. Credit cards: MC and V.

Chesapeake House
Tangier Island, Virginia 23440
804-891-2331

Chesapeake House is known for its simple atmosphere and good home cookin'. It guarantees that you won't leave hungry. Specialties include crab cakes, clam fritters, baked Virginia ham, homemade rolls, and pound cake. Open April 15th through October 15th for breakfast, lunch, and dinner.

Circle Inn
Route 413
Crisfield, Maryland 21817
410-968-1969

Specialties here include quality home-cooked food. You'll find a wide selection of platters, steaks, backfin crab cakes, shrimp, roast beef, and home-made meatloaf. Open for breakfast, lunch, and dinner.

Dockside Restaurant
1003 W. Main Street
Crisfield, Maryland 21817
410-968-3464

The Dockside Restaurant is a handy place to know. For one, it's located just 1/2 block from the town dock. Another reason is "the home style cooked meals." The house listing includes appetizers (crab balls), soups (clam chowder), Salads (tuna, chicken, and shrimp). You may also try a hot and hearty sandwich or a combination platter. Open daily for breakfast, lunch and dinner.

Fishermen's Corner
Tangier Island, Virginia 23440
804-891-2571

House specialties include a wide variety of freshly caught seafood featuring hard shell crabs, fish, soft shell crabs, oysters, and clams. Open for lunch and dinner.

Harbor Side Restaurant
Ewell, Maryland 21842
410-425-2201

Harbor Side Restaurant specializes in seafood dishes, corn pudding, homemade pies, homemade rolls, crab cakes, crab soup. Open for lunch and dinner.

Side Street Seafood Market
10th and Main Street
Crisfield, Maryland 21817
410-968-2442

"Best Crabs on the Shore." Raw bar upstairs. Outside wraparound deck offers an extensive view of the Crisfield harbor. Open daily for lunch and dinner.

Restaurants, cont.

The Cove Restaurant
8th and Broadway
Crisfield, Maryland 21817
410-968-COVE

House specialties include surf &
turf, stuffed lobster tail, crab au
gratin, crab imperial, shrimp
creole, and a Chesapeake Bay
feast platter. Open for breakfast,
lunch, and dinner. Credit cards:
MC and V.

Watermen's Inn
9th and Main Street
Crisfield, Maryland 21817
410-968-2119

Casually elegant atmosphere.
The Watermen's Inn specializes
in fresh seafood dishes and char-
coal-broiled steaks. Its location,
only a block from the waterfront, is a nice place to walk to
and enjoy a large assortment of
overstuffed sandwiches and
great breakfasts. Open Monday
through Saturday for breakfast,
lunch, and dinner. Open Sunday for lunch and dinner. Credit
cards: MC and V.

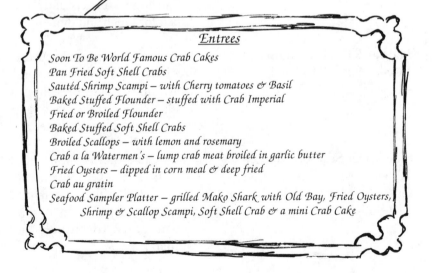

Entrees

Soon To Be World Famous Crab Cakes
Pan Fried Soft Shell Crabs
Sautéd Shrimp Scampi – with Cherry tomatoes & Basil
Baked Stuffed Flounder – stuffed with Crab Imperial
Fried or Broiled Flounder
Baked Stuffed Soft Shell Crabs
Broiled Scallops – with lemon and rosemary
Crab a la Watermen's – lump crab meat broiled in garlic butter
Fried Oysters – dipped in corn meal & deep fried
Crab au gratin
Seafood Sampler Platter – grilled Mako Shark with Old Bay, Fried Oysters,
      Shrimp & Scallop Scampi, Soft Shell Crab & a mini Crab Cake

Accommodations

■ BED AND BREAKFASTS

Bernice Guy Bed and Breakfast
Ewell, Maryland 21824
410-425-2751

Chesapeake House
Tangier Island, Virginia 23440
804-891-2331

Ewell Tide Inn
Ewell, Maryland 21824
410-425-2141

Leonora's Crisfield Inn
209 West Main Street
Crisfield, Maryland 21817
410-968-2181

My Fair Lady
38 Main Street
Crisfield, Maryland 21817
410-968-3514

■ CAMPING

Janes Island State Park
40 Alfred Lawson Drive
Crisfield, Maryland 21817
410-968-1565

■ HOTELS, MOTELS, AND INNS

Paddlewheel Motel
701 West Main Street
Crisfield, Maryland 21817
410-968-2220

Pines Motel
P.O. Box 106
Somerset Avenue
Crisfield, Maryland 21817
410-968-0900

Somer's Cove Motel
RR Norris Drive
Crisfield, Maryland 21817
410-968-1900

SNOW HILL

■ **BACKGROUND:** A walk through Snow Hill is a walk through 300 years of Maryland history. This small settlement was founded by English colonists in 1642 and named Snow Hill after a district in London. The charming hamlet is located on the south bank of the Pocomoke River, whose deep, dark waters are bounded by bald cypress. Together, these features distinguish the Pocomoke as one of the nation's most scenic rivers. Snow Hill boasts of over 100 homes more than 100 years old.

Attractions

■ **VISITOR INFORMATION**

Berlin Chamber of Commerce
Route 50 and 113
Berlin, Maryland 21811
410-641-2700

Ocean City Visitor's Bureau
P.O. Box 116
Ocean City, Maryland 21863
410-289-8181

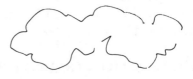

Snow Hill Chamber of Commerce
P.O. Box 176
Snow Hill, Maryland 21863
410-632-0809

Worcester County Tourism
P.O. Box 208
105 Pearl Street
Snow Hill, Maryland 21863
410-632-3617

■ BOAT CRUISES

**Pocomoke River Canoe
Company**
Route 12/Draw Bridge
Snow Hill, Maryland 21863
410-632-3971

If you're looking for a few hours of tranquil canoeing, or a few days of wilderness adventure, you'll find it here on the Pocomoke River. From this River front boathouse, you need only paddle around the bend to find yourself in a natural river paradise. It's an experience for any nature lover. Open weekends in the spring and fall and daily from Memorial Day through Labor Day from 9 a.m. to 5 p.m. Extended hours on weekends and holidays. Closed Mondays except holidays. Fee.

Tillie the Tug
Sturgis Park Dock
Snow Hill, Maryland 21863
800-345-6754
410-632-0680

Cruise the Pocomoke River with local narration on lore, history, and natural wonders of the beautiful Pocomoke River. Cruises are available Wednesday through Sunday, mid-June through Labor Day (schedule subject to change). Fee.

■ HISTORIC SITES:

Furnace Town
Route 12
Snow Hill, Maryland 21863
410-632-2650

Furnace Town is one of the oldest industrial sites in Maryland. It is home to one of the earliest hot-blast mechanisms still intact. Archaeological digs of village visible. Open April to November, Tuesday through Sunday, 10 a.m. to 4 p.m. Admission charge.

■ HISTORIC TOWNS

Berlin
Route 50 and 113
Berlin, Maryland 21811
410-641-2700

Turn-of-the-century commercial district, antique shops, 1895 restored Victorian Atlantic Hotel, Federal-era homes.

Ocean City
U.S. 50
Ocean City, Maryland 21842
410-289-9181

Atlantic seaside resort with accommodations, restaurants, amusements, beach, fishing, boardwalk. Ocean City Convention Hall provides entertainment year round. Free brochure available.

■ MUSEUMS

Mt. Zion One Room Schoolhouse Museum
Ironside Street
Snow Hill, Maryland 21863
410-632-0515

Experience a class as it might have been conducted in the early days, complete with lunch pails, recitation bench, and double slates. Open year round. Free.

Julia A. Purnell Museum
208 West Market Street
Snow Hill, Maryland 21863
410-632-0515

Snow Hill, showcase of Worcester County lore, depicts history from Indian times and the Colonial period up to and including the Victorian era. Open daily, 11 a.m. to 5 p.m. and on Sunday, 1 p.m. to 5 p.m. Admission charge.

Calvin B. Taylor House Museum
North Main Street
Berlin, Maryland 21811
410-641-2700

This restored early 19th century house is now a museum. Open Wednesdays and Fridays, 1 p.m. to 4 p.m. Admission charge.

■ PARKS AND GARDENS

Assateague State and National Seashore Parks
Route 611 at Atlantic Ocean
Ocean City, Maryland 21842
410-641-2120

A barrier island in the Atlantic Ocean, famous for wild ponies that roam free. Abundance of wildlife, nature trails, visitor center. Open sunrise to sunset. Admission charge.

Pocomoke River State Park
3461 Worcester Highway
Snow Hill, Maryland 21863
410-632-2566

Pocomoke River State Forest and Park is available for picnic areas, launch ramps, hunting, swimming pool, crabbing, and three self-guided nature trails. Fee for some services. Baytrippers take note: the park contains Pocomoke Cypress Swamps, one of the northern-most stands of bald cypress in the US. Open sunrise to sunset.

■ SEASONAL EVENTS

Canoe Jousting Championships
Sturgis Park
P.O. Box 176
Snow Hill, Maryland 21863
410-632-0809

A different translation of an old game, this annual event is offered by the town of Snow Hill. Easy viewing from the banks of Sturgis Park. Held noon to 5 p.m. in early August. Free.

Pocomoke River Canoe Challenge
P.O. Box 29
Pocomoke City, Maryland 21851
410-957-1334

This scenic canoe race begins in Sturgis Park in Snow Hill and continues 12 miles down the Pocomoke River to finish at Cypress Park in Pocomoke City. Mid June. Free.

Restaurants

Atlantic Hotel
2 North Main Street
Berlin, Maryland 21811
410-641-3589

The hotel dining room is naturally intimate and filled with the kind of period furnishings and fine china you might want for your dream home. There are such specialties as poached Atlantic salmon, fricassee chicken, roast loin of pork and peppered filet. Open daily for lunch and dinner. Credit cards: MC and V.

Snow Hill Inn
104 E. Market Street
Snow Hill, Maryland 21863
410-632-2102

It seldom snows in Snow Hill but the sun shines bright on the Snow Hill Inn. The crab dishes are considered very special here, including prime rib, broiled scallops, and shrimp scampi. Homemade desserts such as chocolate chip pie are extra rich and extra pleasing. Open Wednesday through Saturday for lunch and dinner, Sundays open dinner only. Credit cards: AE, MC, and V.

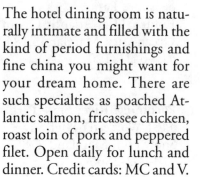

Accommodations

■ BED AND BREAKFASTS

Chanceford Hall
201 Federal Street
Snow Hill, Maryland 21863
410-632-2231

Snow Hill Inn
104 East Market Street
Snow Hill, Maryland 21863
410-632-2102

Holland House
5 Bay Street
Berlin, Maryland 21811
410-641-1956

■ CAMPING

Eagles Nest Campground
12612 Eagles Nest Road
Berlin, Maryland 21811
410-289-9097

Pocomoke River State Park
3461 Worcester Highway
Snow Hill, Maryland 21863
410-632-2566

■ HOTELS, MOTELS, AND INNS

Atlantic Hotel Inn
2 North Main Street
Berlin, Maryland 21811
410-641-3589

The River House Inn
201 East Market Street
Snow Hill, Maryland 21863
410-632-2722

"This faithfully restored 1895 Victorian hotel is the jewel of the Eastern Shore. Placed on the National Register of Historic Places in 1980, the Atlantic Hotel has been carefully restored to its former elegance and grandeur. The hotel is located in the center of Berlin's Historic District; only seven miles from Ocean City and Assateague Island National Seashore. The perfect place for a quiet getaway. One of the...Great Inns of America."

Pocomoke City

■ **BACKGROUND:** Settled in the 1600's on the banks of the Pocomoke River, the name comes from the Indian word, "Pocomoke," meaning "black water." Earlier names for the town were Stevens Ferry, then Meeting House Landing, then Warehouse Landing, then Newtown, until finally in 1878 it became, and remains, Pocomoke City. Baytrippers will enjoy this friendly town. Be sure to take a walk along the river.

Attractions

■ **VISITOR INFORMATION**

Pocomoke City Chamber of Commerce
P.O. Box 113
Pocomoke City, Maryland 21851
410-957-1919

■ **MUSEUMS**

Costen House
Market Street
Pocomoke City, Maryland 21851
410-957-1919

Home of Dr. Isaac T. Costen, first mayor of Pocomoke City. Victorian Italianate architecture, National Register of Historical Sites. Open by appointment. Free.

■ **PARKS AND GARDENS**

Cypress Park
Downtown
Pocomoke City, Maryland 21851

The odd "knees" you will observe protruding above the water in wetland areas belong to the bald cypress. The knees are thought to deliver oxygen to the root system of the swamp loving trees. Park open daily, dawn to dusk. Free.

Restaurants

Don's Seafood
U.S. Route 13 South
Pocomoke City, Maryland 21851
410-957-0177

Swift service and a comfortably relaxed atmosphere complement the innovative seafood selections at Don's. There are featured items as broiled, stuffed shrimp, sauteed soft shell crabs, and pan fried crab cakes as well as several chicken and steak entrees. Open Wednesday through Monday for lunch and dinner. Credit cards: MC and V.

Upper Deck Restaurant
Route 13 South
Pocomoke City, Maryland 21851
410-957-3166

One of Pocomoke City's best-kept secrets. Specialties include crab meat au gratin made with fresh crab meat, baked with a cheddar cheese sauce, and lightly seasoned. Fresh fish of the day—you can have it deep fried or briled in lemon butter. Wonderful corn bread, too. All entrees are served with two vegetables and assorted breads. Open for lunch and dinner. Credit cards: MC and V.

Accommodations

■ **HOTELS, MOTELS, AND INNS**

Days Inn Pocomoke City
Route 13
Pocomoke City, Maryland 21851
410-957-3000

Quality Inn Pocomoke City
U.S. 13 South
Pocomoke City, Maryland 21851
410-957-1300

LOWER BAY

Chincoteague Island to Cape Charles

Follow the water....

- Chincoteague Island
- Onancock
- Wachapreague
- Cape Charles

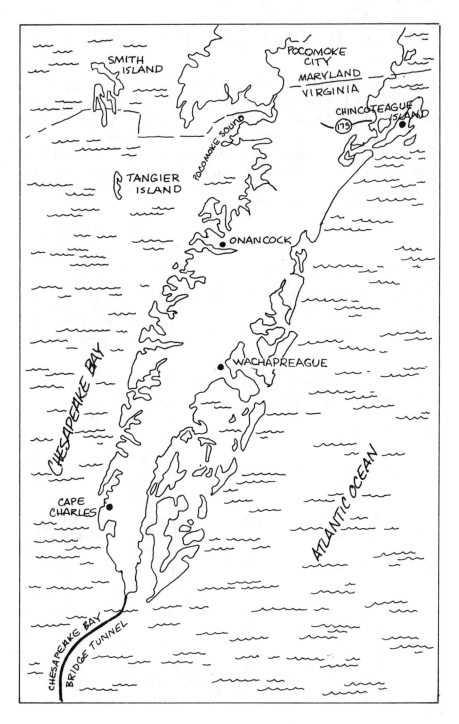

CHINCOTEAGUE ISLAND

■ **BACKGROUND:** The original inhabitants of Chincoteague Island were a tribe of Indians called the Gingo-Teague who named the Island "the beautiful land across the waters." This island is 7 miles long and 1 1/2 half miles wide, and it is connected to the mainland of Virginia's eastern shore by six bridges. An 1800 census revealed 60 full-time residents; today visitors flock year round to Chincoteague to witness nature in all its glory. Bird and wildlife sanctuaries provide unparalleled opportunities for viewing.

Attractions

■ **VISITOR INFORMATION**

Chincoteague Chamber of Commerce
6733 Maddox Boulevard
Chincoteague, Virginia 23336
804-336-6161

Eastern Shore Chamber of Commerce
19056 Industrial Parkway
Melfa, Virginia 23410
804-787-2460

New Church Welcome Center
U.S. 13
P.O. Box 215
New Church, Virginia 23415
804-824-5000

WILDLIFE TOURS

SIGN UP AT THE WILDLIFE REFUGE VISITOR CENTER (804) 336-6155

■ **BOAT CHARTERS**

Chincoteague Charters
3800 South Main Street
Chincoteague, Virginia 23336
804-336-1459
410-437-2287

Daily charters are available aboard the "Pattie Wagon" or the "Proud Mary." Fish for flounder, bluefish, shark, dolphin, and tuna. Call Captain Dwight Daniel for your personalized tour. Seasonal. Fee.

■ BOAT CRUISES

Island Cruises
7058 Maddox Boulevard
Chincoteague, Virginia 23336
804-336-5511

Along the east coast dozens of barrier islands protect the mainland from the fury of the ocean a good way to learn about the areas secrets is to take an island cruise. Baytrippers will tour the south end of the island and out to where the ocean joins with the Bay. Seasonal cruises depart 4 p.m. on Tuesday and Thursday and 6 p.m. on Saturday. Admission charge.

■ BOAT RENTALS

R and R Boat Rental
4183 Main Street
Chincoteague, Virginia 23336
804-336-5465

Bait and tackle, boats and motors, all your fishing and crabbing needs. Open daily for full-day or half-day rentals. Fee.

Snug Harbor
7536 East Side Drive
Chincoteague, Virginia 23336
804-336-6176

These boat rentals are for the serious fisherman or for those who aren't so serious who might enjoy a trip to a secluded beach. The boats are the nicest and most dependable boats on the Island. I think you'll agree. Fee.

Fish Tales
6531 Maddox Boulevard
Chincoteague, Virginia 23336
804-336-3474

Bait and tackle shop—it's all here. Seafood market and charter fishing boats. Call for your personalized tour. Seasonal. Fee.

CHARTER BOATS— FISHING SUPPLIES
WEDNESDAY NIGHT 🦀 CRAB RACES

■ MUSEUMS

NASA Visitor Center
Route 175
Wallops Island, Virginia 23337
804-824-1344

Wallops Flight Facility was the site of some of NASA's early rocket launchings. Today visitors can see a collection of space crafts, relevant videos, and space programs. Open daily during July through August, Thursday through Monday, from 10 a.m. to 4 p.m. Free.

Oyster Museum of Chincoteague
7125 Maddox Boulevard
Chincoteague, Virginia 23336
804-336-6117

The Oyster and Maritime Museum features live marine exhibits, clams, oysters, crabs, starfishes, sea horses, and other marine specimens. Features include historic and maritime artifacts, shell specimens, and implements of the seafood industry. Open daily from Memorial Day weekend to Labor Day, 10 a.m. to 5 p.m.; weekends only during the off season. Admission charge.

Refuge Waterfowl Museum
7059 Maddox Boulevard
Chincoteague, Virginia 23336
804-336-5800

Exhibitions on the watermen's way of life—duck decoys, weapons, boats, etc. Open daily from 10 a.m. to 5 p.m. Closed January and February. Admission charge.

■ PARKS AND GARDENS

Assateague Island National Seashore
Toms Cove/Visitor Center
8663 Beach Road
Chincoteague, Virginia 23336
804-336-6577

Protecting Chincoteague Island from the Atlantic Ocean, Assateague Island boasts 37 miles of the widest and most beautiful beaches on the east coast. A wide variety of nature activities and many miles of unspoiled beaches and sand dunes are yours to explore. Baytrippers should bring their own food and drink as Island facilities are limited to bath houses only. Visitor Center is open daily from 9 a.m. to 4 p.m. Admission charge.

Chincoteague National Wildlife Refuge
8259 Beach Road
Chincoteague, Virginia 23336
804-336-6122

Bicycle trails, fishing, hiking trails, self-guided trails, visitor center. Open daily from 9 a.m. to 5 p.m., except Thursday. Admission charge.

■ SEASONAL EVENTS

Chincoteague Easter Decoy Festival
P.O. Box 258
Chincoteague, Virginia 23336
804-336-6161

This festival is held at the elementary and high school gymnasiums on the island. Gunning decoys are the focus of the competition, and entries come from Maine to California. There are contests for decoys of working shore birds and five categories of decorative miniatures. Following the judging, there is an auction that offers unique works of art donated by the festival's exhibitors. This event is held in early April. Admission charge.

Seasonal Events, cont.

Firemen's Annual Pony Swim and Auction
P.O. Box 258
Chincoteague, Virginia 23336
804-336-6161

Legend tells us that in the 16th century, a Spanish ship carrying a cargo of Spanish mustangs was wrecked off of the coast of Assateague Island. The ponies that we see today may be descendants of those that survived the mishap. The ponies roam free and are the property of the Chincoteague Fire Department. Once a year, volunteer fire fighters round up the ponies and herd them across the quarter-mile Assateague Channel. The auction of the ponies nets thousands of dollars for the Fire Department. Because of the popularity of the event, many families make plans to attend a year in advance. Held on the last Wednesday and Thursday in July. Free.

Oyster Festival
6742 Maddox Boulevard
Chincoteague, Virginia 23336
804-336-3111
804-336-6161

The annual oyster festival is held at the Maddox Family Campground on Columbus Day weekend. Its menu includes oyster fritters, raw oysters, steamed oysters, fried oysters, clam fritters, cole slaw, potato salad, hush puppies, hot dogs, and more. Tickets are limited for this all-you-can-eat event. Baytrippers, sign up early! Held in early October, 12 noon to 4 p.m. Admission charge.

Seafood Festival
Tom's Cove Park
8128 Beebe Road
Chincoteague, Virginia 23336
804-336-6498

The annual Seafood Festival has become a ritual for seafood lovers from the surrounding area and for visitors alike. Specialties include half shell clams, oysters, fried clams, and clam fritters. Fried fish is prepared and served fresh from 1 p.m. to 4 p.m. Tickets are required and often sell in advance for this event. Be sure to plan early. Held on the first Wednesday in May. Admission charge.

Restaurants

Like much else on Chincoteague Island, the restaurants are unpretentious and genuinely appealing. As should be the case in a local economy based on fishing, most restaurants boast an impressive seafood selection. The crabs and oysters on your table were likely caught that morning.

AJ's on the Creek
6585 Maddox Boulevard
Chincoteague Island, Virginia 23336
804-336-5888

This restaurant, surrounded by herb gardens and wildlife from Eel Creek, presents a casually elegant atmosphere. Surround yourself in lace, candlelight, and mahogany. Specials include seafood, pasta, veal, steaks, and a fine wine list. Open daily for lunch and dinner; Sunday, dinner only. Credit cards: AE, MC, and V.

Restaurants, cont.

The Beachway Restaurant
6455 Maddox Boulevard
Chincoteague Island, Virginia
23336
804-336-5590

A large garden room menu includes such specialties as rack of lamb, paella, and bouillabaisse. Open for breakfast, lunch, and dinner. Closed Tuesday. Credit cards: AE, DC, MC, and V.

Bill's Seafood Restaurant
4040 Main Street
Chincoteague Island, Virginia
23336
804-336-5831

Bill's offers a "native seafood" menu which includes a wide variety of items in addition to local seafood. You'll also find sandwiches, chicken, sirloin, and pork chops. Open daily for breakfast, lunch, and dinner.

Chincoteague Inn
6262 Marlin Street
Chincoteague Island, Virginia
23336
804-336-6110

Great open-air lunch spot with fish dinners that highlight the Chincoteague fishing corridor. Drum, shark, tuna, monkfish, and flounder-the list goes on. Open daily for lunch and dinner. Credit cards: MC and V.

Don's Seafood Restaurant
North Main Street
Chincoteague Island, Virginia
23336
804-336-5715

A casual, yet tasteful atmosphere allows you "to get down" to eating mouth-watering crab specialties and wonderful fish and chips. Open daily for breakfast, lunch, and dinner.

Etta's Family Restaurant
East Side Drive
Chincoteague, Virginia 23336
804-336-5644

At Etta's everything is cooked to order. Try the cream of crab soup and a hot beef sandwich with french fries and gravy. Open daily for breakfast, lunch, and dinner. Credit cards: D, MC, and V.

— EAT —

Landmark Crabhouse
Main Street/Landmark Plaza
Chincoteague, Virginia 23336
804-336-5552

The Landmark Crabhouse commands a stunning Bay view and a stupendous menu that includes crabs, oysters, shrimp, and char-broiled steak. Open Monday through Saturday for dinner and Sunday for lunch and dinner. Closed Monday during the winter. Credit cards: MC and V.

Pony Pines Restaurant
East Side Drive
Chincoteague, Virginia 23336
804-336-9746

The Pony Pines Restaurant is not only one of the oldest restaurants on the island; many feel it's the best. Suggested choices are fresh fish of the day or any of the crab dishes. Open daily for lunch and dinner. Credit cards: MC and V.

Shucking House Restaurant
Main Street/Landmark Plaza
Chincoteague Island, Virginia
23336
804-336-5145

The Shucking House offers a splendid view of the boats and trawlers that ply the channel on the Chincoteague Bay. Specialties include oysters and clams, cream of crab soup, crab cakes, and crab imperial as well as catch-of-the-day. Open daily for breakfast, lunch, and dinner. Credit cards: AE, D, MC, and V.

Wright's Seafood Restaurant
Atlantic Road
Atlantic, Virginia 23337
804-824-4012

Specials include steamed crabs and shrimp, Alaskan king crabs, and BBQ'd ribs. Open daily for dinner. Credit cards: AE, MC, and V.

Accommodations

Baytrippers can choose a cozy cottage, a charming Victorian inn on the Bay, or a gracious, elegant, and romantic antebellum bed and breakfast furnished with antiques. It's a great way to travel on the shore and enjoy the comforts of home.

■ BED AND BREAKFASTS

Garden and the Sea Inn
Route 710
New Church, Virginia 23415
804-824-0672

Miss Molly's Inn
113 Main Street
Chincoteague, Virginia 23336
804-336-6686

Little Traveller Island Manor House
North Main Street
Chincoteague, Virginia 23336
804-336-5436

The Watson House
4240 Main Street
Chincoteague, Virginia 23336
804-336-1564

The Main Street House
4356 Main Street
Chincoteague, Virginia 23336
804-336-6030

Year of the Horse Inn
600 South Main Street
Chincoteague, Virginia 23336
804-336-3221

■ CAMPING

Maddox Family Campground
6742 Maddox Boulevard
Chincoteague, Virginia 23336
804-336-3111

Tom's Cove Campground
8128 Beebe Road
Chincoteague, Virginia 23336
804-336-6498

■ HOTELS, MOTELS, AND INNS

Assateague Inn
39B Seashell Drive
Chincoteague, Virginia 23336
804-336-3738

Lighthouse Motel
224 North Main Street
Chincoteague, Virginia 23336
804-336-5091

Chincoteague Motor Lodge
Taylor Street at Deep Hole Road
Chincoteague, Virginia 23336
804-336-6415

Mariner Motel
6273 Maddox Boulevard
Chincoteague, Virginia 23336
804-336-6565

Driftwood Motor Lodge
7105 Maddox Boulevard
Chincoteague, Virginia 23336
804-336-6557

Refuge Motor Inn
7058 Maddox Boulevard
Chincoteague, Virginia 23336
804-336-5511

Duck Haven Cottages
6582 Church Street
Chincoteague, Virginia 23336
804-336-6290

Waterside Motor Inn
544 South Main Street
Chincoteague, Virginia 23336
804-336-3434

Island Motor Inn
4391 Main Street
Chincoteague, Virginia 23336
800-832-2925

ONANCOCK

■ **BACKGROUND:** The Algonquian Indians called it "a foggy place." They maintained a settlement here until around 1670. In 1680, Onancock became a port of entry. The land was purchased from Charles Scarburgh and was first called Port Scarburgh. By 1690 it was called Onancock Town. Onancock today is the second largest community on the Eastern Shore of Virginia.

Attractions

■ **VISITOR INFORMATION**

Eastern Shore of Virginia Chamber of Commerce
P.O. Drawer R
Melfa, Virginia 23410
804-787-2460

■ **BOAT CRUISES**

Tangier Island Cruise
The Wharf
Onancock, Virginia 23417
804-787-8220

Cruise to scenic Tangier Island which lies in the center of the Chesapeake Bay. Named in 1608 by Captain John Smith and settled in 1686, this island maintains a way of life almost three centuries old. From Onancock, it's 16 miles into the Bay to Tangier Island. Open daily, June 1 to September 30. Depart from Onancock at 10 a.m. and arrive at Tangier at 11 a.m. Depart from Tangier at 1:30 p.m. and arrive at Onancock at 2:45 p.m. Fee.

■ HISTORIC TOWNS

Accomac
Route 13
Accomac, Virginia 23301
804-787-2460

Accomac is a walking town; it's small and compact. The town has a sprinkling of colonial charm, highlighted with tree-shaded streets, pretty gardens, and well-tended lawns. Park in the center of town at the Court-house Green and begin your visit with a stop at the Debtor's Prison, the Courthouse, and the Victorian Clerk's Office.

■ MUSEUMS

Eastern Shore Railway Museum
18468 Dunne Street
Parksley, Virginia 23421
804-665-4618

The museum contains the restored railroad station on the original site of the old Parksley Station. Railroad memorabilia and relics are on display. Open Tuesday through Saturday from 10:30 a.m. to 4 p.m. and Sunday from 1 p.m. to 4 p.m. Admission charge.

Hopkins and Bros. Store
The Wharf
Onancock, Virginia 23417
804-787-4478

One of the oldest general stores on the east coast. Merchandise ranges from groceries to dry goods to local arts and crafts. Registered landmark store, circa 1842.

Kerr Place
69 Market Street
Onancock, Virginia 23417
804-787-8012

Historic, elegant, restored mansion. This was the 1799 home of a Scottish merchant. Open from March through December, Tuesday through Saturday, 10 a.m. to 4 p.m. Admission charge.

Museums, cont.

Locustville Academy
Route 605
Locustville, Virginia 23404
804-787-4826

The Locustville Academy building was opened in 1859 and offered classes for those who planned to enter college or business professions. Today a small museum is housed in the building. Open by appointment. Free.

Restaurants

The Hungrey Duck
57 Market Street
Onancock, Virginia
804-787-8700

The Hungrey Duck's bright contemporary interior is the setting for healthful salads, steamship round of beef, "add on" hamburgers and homemade desserts. But there's much, much more. Open Tuesday through Saturday for breakfast, lunch and dinner. Open Sunday for brunch. Credits cards MC and V.

Market Street Inn
47 Market Street
Onancock, Virginia 23417
804-787-7626

The locals flock to the Market Street Inn for crab cakes, prime ribs, meat loaf, and chicken with dumplings. My favorite dish is flounder stuffed with crab meat. Open for breakfast, lunch and dinner. Credit cards: D, DC, MC, and V.

Owl Restaurant
U.S. Route 13
Parksley, Virginia 23421
804-665-5191

Locals rate the spoonbread served here to be the best in the State. While their chicken is panfried, I still opt for the crab cakes. Don't forget to try the homemade desserts. Open daily for breakfast, lunch, and dinner. Credit cards: D, MC, and V.

Accommodations

■ BED AND BREAKFASTS

Colonial Manor Inn B&B
84 Market Street
Onancock, Virginia 23417
804-787-3521

Spinning Wheel
31 North Street
Onancock, Virginia 23417
804-787-7311

■ HOTELS, MOTELS, AND INNS

Anchor Motel
Route 13
Onley, Virginia 23418
804-442-6363

Evergreen Inn
Muirs Path
Pungoteague, Virginia 23422
804-442-3375

Budget Host Motel
Route 13
Onley, Virginia 23418
804-787-8000

Pungoteague Junction B&B
30230 Bobtown Road
Pungoteague, Virginia 23422
804-442-3581

Captain's Quarters Motel
Route 13
Melfa, Virginia 23410
804-787-4545

Owl Motel
Route 13
Parksley, Virginia 23421
804-665-5191

Comfort Inn
Route 13
Onley, Virginia 23418
804-787-7787

Whispering Pines
Route 13
Accomac, Virginia 23301
804-787-1300

WACHAPREAGUE

■ **BACKGROUND:** In the language of the Indians, Wachapreague translates to "Little City by the Sea." Today Wachapreague is the "flounder fishing capital of the world" and on any given day hundreds of boats search here for this tasty fish.

Attractions

■ **VISITOR INFORMATION**

Eastern Shore of Virginia Chamber of Commerce
P.O. Drawer R
Melfa, Virginia 23410
804-787-2460

■ **BOAT CHARTERS**

Wachapreague Boat Association
Wachapreague Marina
Wachapreague, Virginia 23480
804-787-4110

The bays around Wachapreague yield excellent catches of flounder. In addition to inshore fishing for most of the species found in the Bay, the local marinas feature offshore fishing. Surf fishing may not yield the greatest catches, but there is little that is more pleasant than spending the day on the beach. Seasonal. Fee.

■ **BOAT CRUISES**

Barrier Island Cruises
Island House Dock
Wachapreague, Virginia 23480
804-787-2105

Skim out to the islands aboard the Skimmer I, a 32-foot pontoon boat. Cruise times are 10 a.m., 2 p.m., and 7 p.m. Other cruise times available by reservation. Fee.

■ MISCELLANEOUS

Bird Watching Tour
Main Street
Wachapreague, Virginia 25480
804-787-2105

Birding tours take you into marshes and back bays. Travel by boat or van, depending on the weather. Wachapreague is located on the Atlantic Flyway, and over 250 species of birds can be admired throughout the year. Sign up for a tour or purchase a package including meals and lodging. Fee.

Butter Beans

Just a bowl of butter beans
Pass the cornbread if you please   (chorus)
I don't want no collard greens
All I want is a bowl of butter beans.

Just a piece of country ham
Pass the butter and the jam
Pass the biscuits if you please
And some more of them good old butter beans.

Bread and gravy is alright
Turnip sandwich a delight
But my children all still scream
For another bowl of butter beans.

When they lay my bones to rest
Place a rose upon my chest
And no bloomin' evergreens
All I want is a bowl of butter beans.

(Repeat chorus)

See that woman standing there
With her hands up in the air
She's not pregnant as it seems
She's just full of butter beans.

Gilda Hinman
Parksley, VA

Restaurants

Island House Restaurant
Atlantic Avenue
Wachapreague, Virginia 23480
804-787-4242

Since 1902, a house specialty here has been the clam fritter. Other offerings include fabulous fish dinners, stuffed flounder, steamed oysters, and oysters on the half shell. Open for dinner only on Monday through Saturday, and open on Sunday from 12 noon to 9 p.m. Credit cards: MC and V.

The Trawler Restaurant
Route 13
Exmore, Virginia 23350
804-442-2092

The Trawler is a nautical-themed restaurant that's popular with families and couples. You'll enjoy good food and Dinner Theater productions. Credit Cards: MC and V.

E.L. Willis Restaurant
4456 Willis Wharf Road
Willis Wharf, Virginia 23486
804-442-4225

E.L. Willis Restaurant is housed in the historic old Willis & Co. Store, built in 1850. The original building still maintains its early charm. Baytrippers who take the extra time to search out this peaceful fishing village will be rewarded with tasteful clam fritters. Two Willis Wharf clam fritters, sandwiched between two slices of delicious home-baked bread. The results are mighty good. Open Tuesday through Thursday for breakfast and lunch. Open Friday and Saturday for breakfast, lunch and dinner.

That old clam chowder down
on Wachapreague,
is much better
than on Chincoteague.
Eat it once or twice and
love it all your life.
That old clam chowder down
on Wachapreague.
Gila Hinman
Parksley, VA

Accommodations

■ BED AND BREAKFASTS

Ballard House
Route 660
Willis Wharf, Virginia 23486
804-442-2206

Burton House
11 Brooklyn Street
Wachapreague, Virginia 23480
804-787-4560

■ HOTELS, MOTELS, AND INNS

Hotel Wachapreague
Box 360 - Main Street
Wachapreague, Virginia 23480
804-787-2105

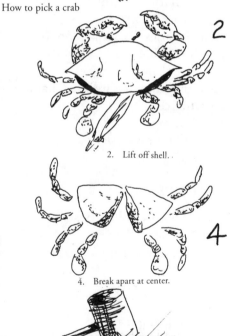

How to pick a crab

1. Lift apron.

2. Lift off shell.

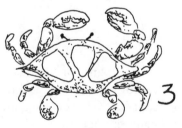

3. Scrape off feathery gills.

4. Break apart at center.

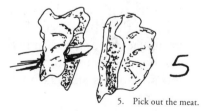

5. Pick out the meat.

CAPE CHARLES

■ **BACKGROUND:** The town of Cape Charles was named for the nearby cape at the entrance to the Chesapeake Bay. Cape Charles was established in 1884 when the New York, Philadelphia, and Norfolk Railroad extended its line from Philadelphia to Norfolk. The town grew rapidly, and many large homes were constructed for railroad executives. Many of the structures came into being between 1885 and 1920. Most of the town is now a Historic District, and many of the homes have been restored.

Attractions

■ **VISITOR INFORMATION**

Cape Charles Chamber of Commerce
P.O. Box 87
Cape Charles, Virginia 23310
804-331-2304

Eastern Shore of Virginia Chamber of Commerce
P.O. Drawer R
Melfa, Virginia 23410
800-787-2460

■ **BEACHES**

Cape Charles Public Beach
Bay Avenue
Cape Charles, Virginia 23310

The wide expanse of white sand is ideal for sunbathing, and the adjacent Bay waters are shallow and calm enough to be safe for small children. The mile-long seawall promenade, known locally as the "Boardwalk," is a great place for a stroll. Sit in the gazebo, and watch some of the most fabulous sunsets on the east coast.

■ BOAT CHARTERS

Cape Charles Fishing Center, Inc.
One Marina Road
Cape Charles Harbor
Cape Charles, Virginia 23310
804-331-4400
804-331-2601

For more than three centuries, watermen have been working the fishing grounds of the Chesapeake. Now you can, too! For an exciting day on the Bay, sign up with Captain Jim Jenrette. He'll help you snag the big ones. Seasonal operation. Call for your schedule. Fee.

Cherrystone Resort
Route 680
Cheriton, Virginia 23316
804-331-3063

Climb aboard "The Miss Jennifer," and try your hand at Chesapeake Bay drift fishing. The biggest and best fish are right here on the Lower Bay. The 50-foot "Miss Jennifer" is owned and operated by Captain Ray Cardone. It departs from the Cherrystone Dock. Open daily, Memorial Day to Labor Day, 8 a.m. to 12 noon and 1 p.m. to 5 p.m. Fee.

■ CRABBING/FISHING

Kiptopeke State Park
3540 Kiptopeke Drive
Cape Charles, Virginia 23310
804-331-2267
804-786-1712

This park offers a 700-foot-long, lighted fishing pier which is popular with anglers. The pier is open around the clock during fishing season. Sea trout, flounder, spot, croaker, and tautog are frequent catches from the pier. Admission charge.

■ HISTORIC SITES

Custis Tombs
Route 644
Cape Charles, Virginia 23310
804-678-5287

These tombs, dating from the 17th century, are on the site of the original Arlington Plantation, and they contain the remains of John Custis and John Custis IV, Masters of Arlington. The Custis family is linked to the Washington and Lee families.

■ HISTORIC TOWNS

Eastville
Route 13
Eastville, Virginia 23347
804-678-0465

Baytrippers who are history buffs will find a stop at Eastville particularly interesting. The oldest continuous court records (from 1632) in America are here in the Clerk's Office and can be examined. There's also a Debtor's Prison and a Courthouse complex. Open on Monday through Friday, 9 a.m. to 5 p.m. Free.

Oyster
Route 639
Oyster, Virginia 23419

A quaint, waterside village once devoted to seafood production. The homes are modest and are clustered around the one-room Post Office.

■ MISCELLANEOUS

Chesapeake Bay Bridge and Tunnel
P.O. Box 111/Route 13
Cape Charles, Virginia 23310
804-624-3511

One of the engineering wonders of the world, the Chesapeake Bay Bridge-Tunnel connects the eastern shore of Virginia to the mainland. The route literally takes you to the sea! It strides out boldly where the Bay meets the Atlantic Ocean, and for 17.6 miles takes you over and under the waves. The southernmost of the four man-made islands include a restaurant and a free fishing pier. Fee.

Crennar's Country Store
213 Mason Avenue
Cape Charles, Virginia 23310
804-331-1488

The local antique dealer's private collection is on display in this turn-of-the-century store. Apply for admission at the antique shop next door. Free.

Eastern Shore of Virginia National Wildlife Refuge Museum
Route 600
Cape Charles, Virginia 23310
804-331-2760

Established by the Department of Interior and open to the public. Exhibits and nature trails are available. Open daily from 10 a.m. to 4 p.m. Free.

■ PARKS AND GARDENS

Eyre Hall
Route 636
Eastville, Virginia 23310

Eyre Hall is a Virginia historical landmark and one of the Eastern Shore's finest homes. The house is not open to the public but the gardens are. Baytrippers note: The gardens are a geometrically arranged pattern of yew, boxwood, crepe myrtle, and magnolia. Open daily. Free.

Kiptopeke State Park
3540 Kiptopeke Drive
Cape Charles, Virginia 23310
804-331-2267

Kiptopeke Beach was named in honor of the younger brother of the King of the Accawmack Indians who befriended early settlers. Kiptopeke means "Big Water." This State Park offers swimming (lifeguards from Memorial Day to Labor Day), a fishing pier, and hiking trails. Open daily from 8 a.m. to 6 p.m. Fee.

■ SEASONAL EVENTS

Cape Charles Crab Festival
Town Dock
Cape Charles, Virginia 23310
804-331-2304

Live music, clams, crab cakes, crabs by the dozen, and more. Late August. Admission charge.

Eastern Shore Birding Festival
Route 13
Cape Charles, Virginia 23310
804-331-1776
804-787-2460

The Eastern Shore Birding Festival is sponsored by the Eastern Shore of Virginia Chamber of Commerce, and it is held at the Sunset Beach Inn. The area serves as a critical corridor for migrating songbirds as they funnel into this peninsula on the way south to their winter homes. Events include bird exhibits, art carvings, slide presentations, music, seafood, and more. Held annually, two-day event, early October. Admission charge.

Restaurants

Rebecca's Restaurant
7 Strawberry Street
Cape Charles, Virginia 23310
804-331-3879

Home-cooked, daily specials and fresh seafood are featured in this neighborhood family restaurant. Open daily for breakfast, lunch, and dinner.

Someplace Else Restaurant
U.S. Route 13
Cape Charles, Virginia 23310
804-331-8430

Specialties include prime rib, seafood, steaks, subs, pizza, and munchies. Open daily for lunch and dinner.

Sting-Rays Restaurant
Route 213
Capeville, Virginia 23313
804-331-2505

Sting-Rays Restaurant is conveniently located at the Cape Center. Specialties include prime rib, marinated chicken breast, crab cakes and country ham. Open daily for breakfast, lunch and dinner.

Accommodations

■ BED AND BREAKFASTS

Nottingham Ridge
28184 Nottingham Ridge Lane
Cape Charles, Virginia 23310
804-331-1010

Seagate
9 Tazewell Avenue
Cape Charles, Virginia 23310
804-331-2206

Pickett's Harbor B&B
28288 Goffigon Lane
Cape Charles, Virginia 23310
804-331-2212

Sunset Inn
108 Bay Avenue
Cape Charles, Virginia 23310
804-331-2424

■ CAMPING

Cherrystone Camping Resort
Cherrystone Boulevard
Cheriton, Virginia 23316
804-331-3063

Kiptopeke State Park
3540 Kiptopeke Drive
Cape Charles, Virginia 23310
804-331-2267

■ HOTELS, MOTELS, AND INNS

Anchor Motel
Route 13
Nassawadox, Virginia 23413
804-442-6363

Cape Motel
Route 13
Cape Charles, Virginia 23310
804-331-2461

Days Inn Motel
Route 13
South Cape Charles, Virginia
23310
804-331-1000

Rittenhouse Motor Lodge
Route 13
Cape Charles, Virginia 23310
804-331-2768

Sunset Beach Inn
Route 13
Cape Charles, Virginia 23310
804-331-1776

INDEX

INDEX

INDEX

Parks and Gardens

Seasonal Events

INDEX

Tours

Wildlife Refuges

INDEX

RESTAURANTS

INDEX

ACCOMMODATIONS

Bed and Breakfasts

INDEX

INDEX

ACKNOWLEDGEMENTS

Linda Brudvig
Scott Brudvig
Clevie Clark
Crisfield Bill and Gracie
Leslie Dawson
Mike Dirham
Falls Camera
Jose Garnham
Dean Gore
Louise Jennings
Raymond McAlwee
New Bay Times
Pat Piper
Pica & Points Typography
Robin Quinn
Tab Distributing Co.
Tom Vernon

Cover Design by Denise McDonald

For Other Readers

Blackistone, Mick, *The Day They Left the Bay.*
    Blue Crab Press, 1991.
Warner, William, *Beautiful Swimmers.*
    Little, Brown & Company, 1976.
Lawson, Glenn, *Bay Keeper.*
    Zak Books, 1993.
Footner, Hulbert, *Rivers of the Eastern Shore.*
    Tidewater Publishers, 1972.
Smith, Robert, *Maritime Museums of North America.*
    Naval Institute Press, 1990.
Collings, Francis, *The Discovery of the Chesapeake Bay.*
    Chesapeake Bay Maritime Museum, 1988.
Lippson, Alice and Robert, *Life in the Chesapeake Bay.*
    Johns Hopkins University Press, 1984.

Dize, Frances W., *Smith Island.*
    Tidewater Publishers, 1990.
Shomette, Donald, *Pirates of the Chesapeake.*
    Tidewater Publishers, 1985.
Holly, David C., *Tidewater by Steamboat.*
    Johns Hopkins University Press, 1991.
Fisher, Alan, *Day Trips in Delmarva.*
    Rambler Books, 1992.
Sherwood, John, *Maryland's Vanishing Lives.*
    Johns Hopkins University Press, 1994.
Brait, Susan, *Chesapeake Gold.*
    University Press of Kentucky, 1990.
Kupperman, Karen Ordahl, *Captain John Smith.*
    University of North Carolina Press, 1988.

Walters, Keith, *Chesapeake Stripers*.
Aerie House, 1990.

Corddry, Mary U., *Museums and Monuments of the Eastern Shore of Maryland*.
The Queen Anne Press, 1990.

White, Christopher, *Chesapeake Bay, a Field Guide*.
Tidewater Press, 1989.

Alotta, Robert, *Sign Posts & Settlers*.
Bonus Books, 1992.

Bell, David, *Awesome Chesapeake*.
Tidewater Publishers, 1994.

Blackistone, Mick, *Sunup to Sundown*.
Blue Crab Press, 1991.

Warren, Marion, *Bringing Back the Bay*.
Johns Hopkins University Press, 1994.

Taylor, John, *Birds of the Chesapeake Bay*.
Johns Hopkins University Press, 1992.

For additional information on ordering books or discount schedule, write:

Marian Hartnett Press
Box 51
Friendship Road
Friendship, Maryland 20758

About the Author

Whitey Schmidt, a native Marylander who "lives on the Bay" is author of the popular culinary classic's *The Crab Cookbook* and the *Flavor of the Chesapeake Bay Cookbook*. Other Schmidt selections include, *A Guide to Chesapeake Seafood Dining* and the best selling *The Official Crab Eater's Guide*. The food writer's thoughts on fine dining and tempting meal preparations appear regularly in his syndicated cooking column "Schmidt's Hit's."

About the Illustrator:

Craig Robinson was reared in Baltimore, Maryland. His formal training was developed while attending the Maryland Institute College of Art. His work has appeared in *Scene* Magazine, *The New Bay Times* and *The Capital* Newspaper.

BOOK ORDER FORM

Chesapeake Books Make Excellent Gifts

THE CRAB COOKBOOK
Specialty dishes include:
  Crunchy Crab Nuggets
  New Orleans Crab Spread
  Baltimore Crab Soup
  G.W.'s She Crab Soup
  Crab Meat and Canteloupe Salad
  Chesapeake Bay Crab Salad
  Maryland Crab Cakes
  Oyster House Road Crab Cakes
  Deale Deviled Crab
  Northern Neck Stuffed Crab
  Soft Shell Crabs with Tarragon Sauce
  Spicy Stuffed Soft Shell Crab
  Miles River Crab Imperial
  Choptank Crab Fritters

BAYTRIPPER VOL. I
EASTERN SHORE

BAYTRIPPER VOL. II
WESTERN SHORE
Whitey gives you an insider's tour...town by town throughout the Western Shore of the Chesapeake Bay. Coverage extends to the Bay's Eastern Shore in Volume I. Bay trips, day trips, out-of-the-way trips...you'll find it all here in his two helpful, informative guides!

FLAVOR OF THE CHESAPEAKE BAY COOKBOOK
Whitey's exceptional recipes—some elegant, others informal—are combined with beautiful photographs by the region's foremost photographer, Marion E. Warren, along with historic anecdotes and relevant commentary. Browse through and experience the Chesapeake with pleasure. Or enjoy cooking these savory foods that are sure to delight. You and your guests are in for a flavorful treat!

ORDERED BY: _____
NAME   ADDRESS   CITY, STATE, AND ZIP

SHIP TO: _____
NAME   ADDRESS   CITY, STATE AND ZIP

ITEM NO.	QUANTITY	DESCRIPTION	PRICE	TOTAL	MAIL TO:
01		The Crab Cookbook	$12.95		MARIAN HARTNETT PRESS
02		Flavor of the Chesapeake Bay Cookbook	$13.95		Box 51
03		Baytripper / Eastern Shore	$12.95		Friendship Road
04		Baytripper / Western Shore	$14.95		Friendship, Maryland 20758
		TOTAL			
		Shipping for 1 to 3 books		1.75	
		Maryland Residents add 5% Sales Tax			
		TOTAL ENCLOSED